I0061585

Charles Egbert Craddock

Down the ravine

Charles Egbert Craddock

Down the ravine

ISBN/EAN: 9783742892348

Manufactured in Europe, USA, Canada, Australia, Japa

Cover: Foto ©Thomas Meinert / pixelio.de

Manufactured and distributed by brebook publishing software
(www.brebook.com)

Charles Egbert Craddock

Down the ravine

DOWN THE RAVINE

BY

CHARLES EGBERT CRADDOCK

AUTHOR OF "IN THE TENNESSEE MOUNTAINS," "THE PROPHET OF THE
GREAT SMOKY MOUNTAINS," ETC.

BOSTON
HOUGHTON, MIFFLIN AND COMPANY
New York: 85 Fifth Avenue
The Riverside Press, Cambridge

DOWN THE RAVINE.

CHAPTER I.

THE new moon, a gleaming scimitar, cleft the gauzy mists above a rugged spur of the Cumberland Mountains. The sky, still crimson and amber, stretched vast and lonely above the vast and lonely landscape. A fox was barking in the laurel.

This was an imprudent proceeding on the part of the fox, considering the value of his head-gear. A young mountaineer down the ravine was reminded, by the sharp, abrupt sound, of a premium offered by the State of Tennessee for the scalp and ears of the pestiferous red fox.

All unconscious of the legislation of extermination, the animal sped nimbly along the ledge of a cliff, becoming visible from the ra-

vine below, a tawny streak against the gray
rock. Swift though he was, a jet of red light
flashing out in the dusk was yet swifter. The
echoing crags clamored with the report of a
rifle. The tawny streak was suddenly still.
Three boys appeared in the depths of the ravine and looked up.

"Thar now! Ye can't git him off 'n that
thar ledge, Birt," said Tim Griggs. "The
contrairy beastis could n't hev fund a more ill-
convenient spot ter die ef he hed sarched the
mounting."

"I ain't goin' ter leave him thar, though,"
stoutly declared the boy who still held the
rifle. "That thar fox's scalp an' his two ears
air wuth one whole dollar."

Tim remonstrated. "Look-a-hyar, Birt; ef
ye try ter climb up this hyar bluff, ye 'll git
yer neck bruk, sure."

Birt Dicey looked up critically. It was a
rugged ascent of forty feet or more to the narrow ledge where the red fox lay. Although
the face of the cliff was jagged, the rock
greatly splintered and fissured, with many

ledges, and here and there a tuft of weeds or a stunted bush growing in a niche, it was very steep, and would afford precarious foothold. The sunset was fading. The uncertain light would multiply the dangers of the attempt. But to leave a dollar lying there on the fox's head, that the wolf and the buzzard might dine expensively to-morrow!

" An' me so tried for money ! " he exclaimed, thinking aloud.

Nate Griggs, who had not before spoken, gave a sudden laugh, — a dry, jeering laugh.

" Ef all the foxes on the mounting war ter hold a pertracted meet'n, jes' ter pleasure youuns, thar would n't be enough scalps an' ears 'mongst 'em ter make up the money ye hanker fur ter buy a horse."

To buy a horse was the height of Birt's ambition. His mother was a widow; and as an instance of the fact that misfortunes seldom come singly, the horse on which the family depended to till their scanty acres died shortly after his owner. And so, whenever the spring opened and the ploughs all over the country-

side were starting, their one chance to culti-
vate a crop was to hire a mule from their
nearest neighbor, the tanner. Birt was the
eldest son, and his mother had only his work
to offer in payment. The proposition always
took the tanner in what he called a "jubious
time." Spring is the season for stripping the
trees of their bark, which is richer in tannin
when the sap flows most freely, and the mule
was needed to haul up the piles of bark from
out the depths of the woods to the tanyard.
Then, too, Jubal Perkins had his own crops to
put in. As he often remarked in the course
of the negotiation, "I don't eat tan bark —
nor yit raw hides." Although the mule was a
multifarious animal, and ploughed and worked
in the bark-mill, and hauled from the woods,
and went long journeys in the wagon or under
the saddle, he was not ubiquitous, and it was
impossible for him to be in the several places
in which he was urgently needed at the same
time. Therefore, to hire him out on these
terms seemed hardly an advantage to his master. Nevertheless, this bargain was annually

struck. The poverty-stricken widow always congratulated herself upon its conclusion, and it never occurred to her that the amount of work that Birt did in the tanyard was a disproportionately large return for the few days that the tanner's mule ploughed their little fields.

Birt, however, was beginning to see that a boy to drive that mule around the bark-mill was as essential as the mule himself. As Providence had failed to furnish the tanner with a son for this purpose — his family consisting of several small daughters — Birt supplied a long-felt want.

The boy appreciated that his simple mother was over-reached, yet he could not see that she could do otherwise. He sighed for independence, for a larger opportunity. As he drove the mule round the limited circuit, his mind was far away. He anxiously canvassed the future. He cherished fiery, ambitious schemes, — often scorched, poor fellow, by their futility. With his time thus mortgaged, he thought his help to his mother was far less

than it might be. But until he could have a
horse of his own, there was no hope — no
progress. And for this he planned, and
dreamed, and saved.

Partly these considerations, partly the love
of adventure, and partly the jeer in Nate's
laugh determined him not to relinquish the
price set upon the fox's head. He took off his
coat and flung it on the ground beside his
rifle. Then he began to clamber up the cliff.

The two brothers, their hands in the pockets of their brown jeans trousers, stood watching his ascent. Nate had sandy hair, small
gray eyes, set much too close together, and a
sharp, pale, freckled face. Tim seemed only
a mild repetition of him, as if Nature had
tried to illustrate what Nate would be with
a better temper and less sly intelligence.

Birt was climbing slowly. It was a difficult
matter. Here was a crevice that would hardly
admit his eager fingers, and again a projec-
tion so narrow that it seemed to grudge him
foothold. Some of the ledges, however, were
wider, and occasionally a dwarfed huckleberry

bush, nourished in a fissure, lifted him up like a helping hand. He quaked as he heard the roots strain and creak, for he was a pretty heavy fellow for sixteen years of age. They did not give way, however, and up and up he went, every moment increasing the depth below him and the danger. His breath was short; his strength flagged, he slipped more than once, giving himself a great fright; and when he reached the ledge where the dead fox lay, he thought, " The varmint don't wuth it."

Nevertheless he whooped out his triumph to Nate and Tim in a stentorian halloo, for they had already started homeward, and presently their voices died in the distance. Birt faced about and sat down on the ledge to rest, his feet dangling over the depths beneath.

It was a lonely spot, walled in by the mountains, and frequented only by the deer that were wont to come to lick salt from the briny margin of a great salt spring far down the ravine. Their hoofs had worn a deep excavation around it in the countless years and generations that they had herded here. The "lick," as such places are called in Tennessee, was nearly two acres in extent, and in the centre of the depression the brackish water stood to the depth of six feet or more. Birt looked down at it, thinking of the old times when, according to tradition, it was the stamping ground of buffalo as well as deer. The dusk deepened. The shadows were skulking in and out of the wild ravine as the wind rose and fell. They took to his fancy the form of herds of the banished bison, revisiting in this impalpable guise the sylvan shades where they are but a memory now.

Presently he began the rugged descent, considerably hampered by the fox, which he carried by the tail. He stopped to rest whenever he found a ledge that would serve as a seat. Looking up, high above the jagged summit of the cliff that sharply serrated the zenith, he saw the earliest star, glorious in the crimson and amber sky. Below, a point of silver light quivered, reflected in the crimson and amber waters of the "lick." The fire-flies were flickering among the ferns; he saw about him their errant gleam. The shadowy herds trooped down the mountain side.

Now and then his weight uprooted a bush in his hands, and the clods fell. He missed his footing as he neared the base, and came down with a thump. It was a gravelly spot where he had fallen, and he saw in a moment that it was the summer-dried channel of a mountain rill. As he pulled himself up on one elbow, he suddenly paused with dilated eyes. The evening light fell upon a burnished glimmer; — a bit of stone — was it stone? — shining with a metallic lustre.

He looked at it for a moment, his eyes glowing in the contemplation of a splendid possibility.

What were those old stories that his father used to tell of the gold excitement in Tennessee in 1831, when the rich earth flung largess from its hidden wealth along the romantic banks of Coca Creek! Gold had been found in Tennessee — why not here? And once — why not again?

The idea so possessed him that while he was skinning the fox his sharp knife almost sacrificed one of the *two* ears imperatively required by the statute, in order that the wily hunter may not be tempted to present one ear at a time, thus multiplying red foxes and premiums therefor like Falstaff's "rogues in buckram."

He took his way homeward through the darkening woods, carrying the pelt in his hand. It was not long before he could hear the dogs barking, and as he came suddenly upon a little clearing in the midst of the dense, encompassing wilderness, he saw them all trooping down from the unenclosed passage between the two log-rooms which constituted the house. An old hound had half climbed the fence, but as he laid his fore-paw on the topmost rail, his deep-mouthed bay was hushed, — he was recognizing the approaching step of his master. The yellow curs were still insisting upon a marauder theory. One of them barked defiance as he thrust his head between the rails of the fence. There was another head thrust through too, about on a level with Towser's, but it was not a dog's head. As Birt caught a glimpse of it, he called out hastily, " Stand back thar, Tennessee!" And then it was lost to view, for at the sound of his voice all the dogs came huddling over the bars, shrilly yelping a tumultuous welcome.

When Birt had vaulted over the fence, the little object withdrew its head from between the rails and came trotting along beside him, holding up its hand to clasp his.

His mother, standing in the passage, her tall, thin figure distinct in the firelight that came flickering out through the open door, soliloquized querulously : —

" Ef that thar child don't quit that fool way o' stickin' her head a-twixt the rails ter watch fur her brother, she 'll git cotched thar some day like a peeg in a pen, an' git her neck bruk."

Birt overheard her. " Tennessee air too peart ter git herself hurt," he said, a trifle ashamed of his ready championship of his little sister, as a big rough boy is apt to be of gentler emotions.

If ever infancy can be deemed uncouth, she was an uncouth little atom of humanity. Her blue checked homespun dress, graced with big horn buttons, descended almost to her feet. Her straight, awkwardly cropped hair was of a nondescript shade pleasantly called " tow." As she came into the light of the fire, she lifted wide black eyes deprecatingly to her mother.

" She ain't pretty, I know, but she air powerful peart," Birt used to say so often that the phrase became a formula with him.

If she were " powerful peart," it was a fact readily apparent only to him, for she was a silent child, with the single marked characteristic of great affection for her eldest brother and a singular pertinacity in following him about.

" I dunno 'bout Tennie's peartness," his mother sarcastically rejoined.   " 'Pears ter me like the chile hain't never hed good sense; afore she could walk she 'd crawl along the

floor arter ye, an' holler like a squeech-ow*el* ef
ye went off an' lef' her. An' ye air plumb
teched in the head too, Birt, ter set sech store
by Tennie. I look ter see her killed, or
stunted, some day, in them travels o' hern."

For when Birt Dicey went "yerrands" on
the mule through the woods to the Settlement,
Tennessee often rode on the pommel of his
saddle. She followed in the furrow when he
ploughed. She was as familiar an object at
the tanyard as the bark-mill itself. When he
wielded the axe, she perched on one end of the
woodpile. But so far, she had passed safely
through her varied adventures, and gratifying
evidences of her growth were registered on the
door. "Stand back thar, Tennessee!" in a
loud, boyish halloo, was a command when danger was ahead, which she obeyed with the read-
iness of a veteran.

Sometimes, however, this incongruous com-
panionship became irksome to him. Her trust-
ing, insistent affection made her a clog upon
him, and he grew impatient of it.

Ah, little Sister! he learned its value one
day.

The great wood fire was all aflare in the deep chimney-place. Savory odors came from the gridiron and the skillet and the hoe, on the live coals drawn out on the broad hearth. The tow-headed children grew noisy as they assembled around the bare pine table, and began to clash their knives and forks.

Birt, unmindful, crouched by the hearth, silently turning his precious specimens about, that he might examine them by the firelight. Tennessee, her chuffy hand on his shoulder, for she could reach it as he knelt, held her head close to his, and looked at them too with wide black eyes. His mother placed the supper on the table, and twice she called to him to come, but he did not hear. She turned and looked down at him, then broke out sharply in indignant surprise.

"Air ye bereft o' reason, Birt Dicey! Ye set thar nosin' a handful o' rocks ez ef they war fitten ter eat! An' now look at the boy! —a stuffin' 'em in his pockets ter sag 'em down and tear 'em out fur me ter sew in ag'in. Waal, waal! Sol'mon say ef ye spare the

rod ye spile the child — mos' ennybody could
hev fund that out from thar own 'sperience;
but the wisest man that ever lived lef' no
receipt how ter keep a boy's pockets whole
in his breeches."

2

CHAPTER II.

BIRT DICEY lay awake deep into the night, pondering and planning. But despite this unwonted vigil the old bark-mill was early astir, and he went alertly about his work. He felt eager, strong, capable. The spirit of progress was upon him.

The tanyard lay in the midst of a forest so dense that, except at the verge of the clearing, it showed hardly a trace of its gradual despoliation by the industry that nestled in its heart like a worm in the bud. There were many stumps about the margin of the woods, the felled trees, stripped of their bark, often lying among them still, for the supply of timber exceeded the need. In penetrating the wilderness you might mark, too, here and there, a vacant space, where the chestnut-oak, prized for its tannin, had once grown on the slope.

A little log house was in the midst of the
clearing. It had, properly speaking, only one
room, but there was a shed-room attached, for
the purpose of storage, and also a large open
shed at one side. The rail fence inclosed the
space of an acre, perhaps, which was covered
with spent bark. Across the pits planks were
laid, with heavy stones upon them to hold
them in place. A rude roof sheltered the
bark-mill from the weather, and there was the
patient mule, with Birt and a whip to make
sure that he did not fall into reflective pauses
according to his meditative wont. And there,
too, was Tennessee, perched on the lower
edge of a great pile of bark, and gravely
watching Birt.

He deprecated the attention she attracted.
He was sometimes ashamed to have the persis-
tent little sister seen following at his heels like
a midday shadow. He could not know that
the men who stopped and spoke to him and to
her, and laughed at the infirmities of the in-
fant tongue when she replied unintelligibly,
thought better of him for his manifestation of

strong fraternal affection. They said to each
other that he was a "peart boy an' powerful
good ter the t'other chill'en, an' holped the
fambly along ez well ez a man — better 'n thar
dad ever done;" for Birt's father had been
characterized always as "slack-twisted an' onlucky."

The shadows dwindled on the tan. The
winds had furled their wings. White clouds
rose, dazzling, opaque, up to the blue zenith.
The querulous cicada complained in the laurel.
Birt heard the call of a jay from the woods.
And then, as he once more urged the old mule
on, the busy bark-mill kept up such a whir
that he could hear nothing else. He was not
aware of an approach till the new-comer was
close upon him; in fact, the first he knew of
Nate Griggs's proximity was the sight of him.
Nate was glancing about with his usual air
of questioning disparagement, and cracking a
long lash at the spent bark on the ground.

"Hello, Nate!" Birt cried out, eagerly.
"I'm powerful glad ye happened ter kem
hyar, fur I hev a word ter say ter ye."

"I dunno ez I'm minded ter bide," Nate said cavalierly. "I hates to waste time an' burn daylight a-jowin'."

He was still cracking his lash at the ground. There was a sudden, half-articulate remonstrance.

Birt, who had turned away to the bark-mill, whirled back in a rising passion.

"Did ye hit Tennessee?" he asked, with a dangerous light in his eyes.

"No — I never!" Nate protested. "I hain't seen her till this minute. She war standin' a-hint ye."

"Waal, ye skeered her, then," said Birt, hardly appeased. "Quit snappin' that lash. 'Pears-like ter me ez ye makes yerself powerful free round this hyar tanyard."

"Tennie air a-growin' wonderful fast," the sly Nathan remarked pleasantly.

Birt softened instantly. "She air a haffen inch higher 'n she war las' March, 'cordin' ter the mark on the door," he declared, pridefully. "She ain't pretty, I know, but she air powerful peart."

" What war the word ez ye war layin' off ter say ter me?" Nate asked, curiosity vividly expressed in his face.

Birt leaned back against the pile of bark and hesitated. Last night he had thought Nate the most desirable person to whom he could confide his secret whose aid he could secure. There were many circumstances that made this seem wise. But when the disclosure was imminent, something in those small, bead-like eyes, unpleasantly close together, something in the expression of the thin, pale face, something in Nate's voice and manner repelled confidence.

" Nate," said Birt, at last, speaking with that subacute conviction, so strong yet so ill-defined, which vividly warns the ill-judged and yet cannot stop the tongue constrained by its own folly, " what d' ye s'pose I fund in the woods yestiddy?"

The two small eyes, set close together, seemed merged in one, so concentrated was their gaze. Again their expression struck Birt's attention. He hesitated once more.

" Ef I tell ye, will ye promise never ter tell enny livin' human critter ? "

" I hope I may drap stone dead ef I ever tell! " Nate exclaimed.

" I fund a strange metal in the woods yes-tiddy. What d' ye s'pose 't war ? "

Nate shook his head. His breath was quick and he could not control the keen anxiety in his face. A strong flush rose to the roots of his sandy hair, his lips quivered, and his small eyes glittered with greedy expectation. His tongue refused to frame a word.

" *Gold!* " cried Birt, triumphantly.

" Whar be it ? " exclaimed Nate. He was about to start in full run for the spot.

" I ain't agoin' ter tell ye, without we-uns kin strike a trade."

" Waal," said Nate, with difficulty repressing his impatience, " what air you-uns aimin' ter do ? "

" Ye knows ez I hev ter bide hyar with the bark-mill mos'ly, jes' now," said Birt, beginning to expound the series of ideas which he had carefully worked out in his midnight vigil,

" 'kase they hev got ter hev a heap o' tan ter fill them thar vats ag'in. Ef I war ter leave an' go a-gold huntin', the men on the mounting would find out what I war arter, an' they 'd come a-grabblin' thar too, an' mebbe git it all, 'kase I dunno how much or how leetle thar be. I wants ter make sure of enough ter buy a horse, or a mule, or su'thin', ef I kin, 'fore I tells ennybody else. An' I 'lowed ez ye an' me would go pardners. Ye 'd take my place hyar at the tanyard one day, whilst I dug, an' I 'd bide in the tanyard nex' day. An' we would divide fair an' even all we fund."

Nate did not reply. He was absorbed in a project that had come into his head as his friend talked, and the two dissimilar trains of thought combined in a mental mosaic that would have amazed Birt Dicey.

" Ye see," Birt presently continued, " I dunno when I kin git shet o' the tanyard this year. Old Jube Perkins 'lows ez he air mighty busy 'bout'n them hides an' sech, an' he wants me ter holp around ginerally. He say ef I do mo' work 'n I owes him, he 'll make that straight with my mother. An' he declares fur true ef I don't holp him at this junctry, when he needs me, he won't hire his mule to my mother nex' spring; an' ye know it won't do fur we-uns ter resk the corn-crap an' gyarden truck with sech a pack o' chill'n ter vittle ez we-uns hev got at our house."

Nate deduced an unexpected conclusion. "Ye oughter gin me more 'n haffen the make," he said. " 'Kase ef 'twarn't fur me, ye could nt' git none. An' ef ye don't say two thurds, I 'll tell every critter on the mounting an' they 'll be grabblin' in yer gold mine d'rec'ly."

"Ye dunno whar it is," said Birt, quietly.

If a sudden jet from the cold mountain torrent, that rioted through the wilderness down the ravine hard by, had been dashed into Nate's thin, sharp face, he could not have cooled more abruptly. The change almost took his breath away.

"I don't mean *that*, nuther," he gasped with politic penitence, "kase I hev promised not ter tell. I dunno whether I kin holp nohow. I hev got ter do my sheer o' work at home;

we ain't through pullin' fodder off'n our late corn yit."

Birt looked at him in silent surprise.

Nate was older than his friend by several years. He was of an unruly and insubordinate temper, and did as little work as he pleased at home. He often remarked that he would like to see who could make him do what he had no mind to do.

"Mebbe old Jube wouldn't want me round 'bout," he suggested.

"Waal," said Birt, eager again to detail his plans, "he 'lowed when I axed him this mornin' ez he'd be willin' ef I could trade with another boy ter take my place wunst in a while."

Nate affected to meditate on this view of the question. "But it will be toler'ble fur away fur me ter go prowlin' in the woods, a-huntin' fur gold, an' our fodder jes' a-sufferin' ter be pulled. Ef the spot air fur off, I can't come an' I won't, not fur haffen the make."

"'T ain't fur off at all — scant haffen mile,"

replied unwary Birt, anxious to convince. "It air jes' yander nigh that thar salt lick down the ravine. I marks the spot by a bowlder — biggest bowlder I ever see — on the slope o' the mounting."

The instant this revelation passed his lips, regret seized him. "But ye ain't ter go thar 'thout me, ye onderstand, till we begins our work."

"I ain't wantin' ter go," Nate protested. "I ain't sati'fied in my mind whether I'll ondertake ter holp or no. That pullin' fodder ez I hev got ter do sets mighty heavy on my stomach."

"Tim an' yer dad *always* pulls the fodder an' sech — I knows ez that air a true word," said Birt, bluntly. "An' I can't git away from the tanyard at all ef ye won't holp me, 'kase old Jube 'lowed he wouldn't let me swop with a smaller boy ter work hyar; an' all them my size, an' bigger, air made ter work with thar dads, 'ceptin' you-uns."

Nate heard, but he hardly looked as if he did, so busily absorbed was he in fitting this fragment of fact into his mental mosaic. It had begun to assume the proportions of a distinct design.

He suddenly asked a question of apparent irrelevancy.

"This hyar land down the ravine don't b'long ter yer folkses — who do it b'long ter?"

"Don't b'long ter nobody, ye weasel!" Birt retorted, in rising wrath. "D'ye s'pose I'd be a-stealin' of gold off'n somebody else's land?"

Nate's sly, thin face lighted up wonderfully. He seemed in a fever of haste to terminate the conference and get away. He agreed to his friend's proposition and promised to be at the bark-mill bright and early in the morning. As he trudged off, Birt Dicey stood watching the receding figure. His eyes were perplexed, his mind full of anxious foreboding. He hardly knew what he feared. He had only a vague sense of mischief in the air, as slight but as unmistakable as the harbinger of storm on a sunshiny summer day.

"I wisht I hed n't tole him nuthin'," he

said, as he wended his way home that night.
" Ef my mother hed knowed bout'n it all, I
would n't hev been 'lowed ter tell him. She
*de*spises the very sight o' this hyar Nate Griggs
— an' yit she say she dunno why."

After supper he sat gloomy and taciturn in
the uninclosed passage between the two rooms,
watching alternately the fire-flies, as they in-
starred the dark woods with ever-shifting gold
sparks, and the broad, pale flashes of heat
lightning which from time to time illumined
the horizon. There was no motion in the
heavy black foliage, but it was filled with the
shrill droning of the summer insects, and high
in the branches a screech-owl pierced the air
with its keen, quavering scream.

" Tennessee!" exclaimed Birt, as the un-
welcome sound fell upon his ear — " Tennessee! run an' put the shovel in the fire!"

Whether the shovel, becoming hot among
the live coals, burned the owl that was high in
the tree-top outside, according to the country-
side superstition, or whether by a singular co-
incidence, he discovered that he had business

elsewhere, he was soon gone, and the night was left to the chorusing katydids and tree-toads and to the weird, fitful illuminations of the noiseless heat lightning.

Birt Dicey rose suddenly and walked away silently into the dense, dark woods.

"Stop, Tennessee! ye can't go too!" exclaimed Mrs. Dicey, appearing in the doorway just in time to intercept the juvenile excursionist. "Ketch her, Rufus! Ef she would n't hev followed Birt right off in the pitch dark! She ain't afeared o' nothin' when Birt is thar. Git that pomegranate she hed an' gin it ter her ter keep her from hollerin', Rufe; I hed a sight ruther hear the squeech-ow*el.*"

Tennessee, overpowered by disappointment, sobbed herself to sleep upon the floor, and then ensued an interval of quiet. Rufe, a tow-headed boy of ten, dressed in an unbleached cotton shirt and blue-checked homespun trousers, concluded that this moment was the accepted time to count the balls in his brother's shot-pouch. This he proceeded to do, with the aid of the sullen glare from the embers within and the fluctuating gleams of the lightning without. There was no pretense of utility in Rufe's performance; only the love of handling lead could explain it.

"Ye hed better mind," his mother admonished him. "Birt war powerful tried the t'other day ter think what hed gone with his bullets. He'll nose ye out afore long."

"They hev got sech a fool way o' slippin' through the chinks in the floor," said the boy in exasperation. "I never seen the beat! An' thar's no gittin' them out, nuther. I snaked under the house yestiddy an' sarched, an' sarched! — an' I never fund but two. An' Towse, he dragged hisself under thar, too — jes' a-growlin' an' a-snappin'. I thought fur sartin every minit he'd bite my foot off."

He resumed his self-imposed task of counting the rifle balls, and now and then a sharp click told that another was consigned to that limbo guarded by Towse. Mrs. Dicey stood in silence for a time, gazing upon the unutterably gloomy forest, the distant, throbbing stars, and the broad, wan flashes at long intervals gleaming through the sky.

"It puts me in a mighty tucker ter hev yer brother a-settin' out through the woods this hyar way, an' a-leavin' of we-uns hyar, all by ourselves sech a dark night. I'm always afeared thar mought be a bar a-prowlin' round. An' the cornfield air close ter the house, too."

"Pete Thompson — him ez war yander ter the tanyard day 'fore yestiddy with his dad," said the boy, "he tole it ter me ez how he seen a bar las' Wednesday a-climbin' over the fence ter thar cornfield, with a haffen dozen roastin'-ears under his arm an' a watermillion on his head. But *war* it a haffen dozen? I furgits now ef Pete said it war a haffen dozen or nine ears of corn the bar hed;" and he paused to reflect in the midst of his important occupation.

"I'll be bound Pete never stopped ter count 'em," said Mrs. Dicey. "Pick that chile up an' come in. I'm goin' ter bar up the door."

Birt Dicey plodded away through the deep woods and the dense darkness down the ravine.

Although he could not now distinguish one
stone from another, he had an uncontrollable
impulse to visit again the treasure he had discovered. The murmur of the gently bubbling
water warned him of the proximity of the deep
salt spring almost at the base of the mountain,
and, guiding himself partly by the sound, he
made his way along the slope to the great
bowlder beneath the cliffs that served to mark
the spot. As he laid his hand on the bowlder,
he experienced a wonderful exhilaration of
spirit. Once more he canvassed his scheme.
This was the one great opportunity of his
restricted life. Visions of future possibilities
were opening wide their fascinating vistas. He
might make enough to buy a horse, and this
expressed his idea of wealth. "But ef I live
ter git a cent out'n it," he said to himself,
"I'll take the very fust money I kin call my
own an' buy Tennessee a chany cup an' sarcer,
an' a string o' blue beads an' a caliky coat —
ef I die fur it."

His pleased reverie was broken by a sudden
discovery. He was not standing among stones

about the great bowlder; no — his foot had sunk deep in the sand! He stooped down in the darkness and felt about him. The spot was not now as he had left it yesterday afternoon. He was sure of this, even before a fleet, wan flash of the heat lightning showed him at his feet the unmistakable signs of a recent excavation. It was not deep, it was not broad; but it was fresh and it betrayed a prying hand. Again the heat lightning illumined the wide, vague sky. He saw the solemn dark forests; he saw the steely glimmer of the lick; the distant mountains flickered against the pallid horizon; and once more — densest gloom.

CHAPTER III.

It was Nate who had been here, — Birt felt sure of that; Nate, who had promised he would not come.

Convinced that his friend was playing a false part, Birt went at once to the bark-mill in the morning, confident that he would not find Nate at work in the tanyard according to their agreement.

It was later than usual, and Jubal Perkins swore at Birt for his tardiness. He hardly heard; and as the old bark-mill ground and ground the bark, and the mule jogged around and around, and the hot sun shone, and the voices of the men handling the hides at the tanpit were loud on the air, all his thoughts were of the cool, dark, sequestered ravine, holding in its cloven heart the secret he had discovered.

Rufus happened to come to the tanyard to-day. Birt seized the opportunity.

" Rufe," he said, " ye see I can't git away from the mill, 'kase I 'm 'bleeged ter stay hyar whilst the old mule grinds. But ef ye 'll go over yander ter Nate Griggs's house an' tell him ter come over hyar, bein' ez I want to see him partic'lar, I 'll fix ye a squir'l-trap before long ez the peartest old Bushy-tail on the mounting ain't got the gumption ter git out'n. An' let me know ef Nate ain't thar."

Rufe was disposed to parley. He stood first on one foot, then on the other. He cast calculating eyes at the bark-mill and out upon the deep forest. The exact date on which this promise was to be fulfilled had to be fixed before he announced his willingness to set out.

Ten to one, he would have gone without the bribe, had none been suggested, for he loved the woods better than the wood-pile, and a five-mile tramp through its tangles wearied his bones not so much as picking up a single basketful of chips. Some boys' bones are con- stituted thus, strange as it may seem.

So he went his way in his somewhat eccentric gait, compounded of a hop, and a skip,
and a dawdle. He had made about half a
mile when the path curved to the mountain's
brink. He paused and parted the glossy leaves
of the dense laurel that he might look out
over the precipice at the distant heights. How
blue — how softly blue they were! — the end-
less ranges about the horizon. What a golden
haze melted on those nearer at hand, bravely
green in the sunshine! From among the beet-
ling crags, the first red leaf was whirling away
against the azure sky. Even a buzzard had its
picturesque aspects, circling high above the
mountains in its strong, majestic flight. To
breathe the balsamic, sunlit air was luxury,
happiness; it was a wonder that Rufe got on
as fast as he did. How fragrant and cool
and dark was the shadowy valley! A silver
cloud lay deep in the waters of the "lick."
Why Rufe made up his mind to go down
there, he could hardly have said — sheer curiosity, perhaps. He knew he had plenty of
time to get to Nate's house and back before

dark. People who sent Rufe on errands usually reckoned for two hours' waste in each direction. He had no idea of descending the cliffs as Birt had done. He stolidly retraced his way until he was nearly home; then scrambling down rocky slopes he came presently upon a deer-path. All at once, he noticed the footprint of a man in a dank, marshy spot. He stopped and looked hard at it, for he had naturally supposed this path was used only by the woodland gentry.

"Some deer-hunter, I reckon," he said. And so he went on.

With his characteristic curiosity, he peered all around the "lick" when he was at last there. He even applied his tongue, calf-like, to the briny earth; it did not taste so salty as he had expected. As he rolled over luxuriously on his back among the fragrant summer weeds, he caught sight of something in the branches of an oak tree. He sat up and stared. It looked like a rude platform. After a moment, he divined that it was the remnant of a scaffold from which some early settler of

Tennessee had been wont to fire upon the deer
or the buffalo at the "lick," below. Such
relics, some of them a century old, are to be
seen to this day in sequestered nooks of the
Cumberland Mountains. Rufe had heard of
these old scaffolds, but he had never known of
the existence of this one down by the "lick."
He sprang up, a flush of excitement contend-
ing with the dirt on his countenance ; he set
his squirrel teeth resolutely together ; he applied his sturdy fingers and his nimble legs
to the bark of the tree, and up he went like
a cat.

He climbed to the lower branches easily
enough, but he caused much commotion and
swaying among them as he struggled through
the foliage. An owl, with great remonstrant
eyes, suddenly looked out of a hollow, higher
still, with an inarticulate mutter of mingled
reproach, and warning, and anxiety. Rufe
settled himself on the platform, his bare feet
dangling about jocosely. Then, beating his
hands on either thigh to mark the time he
sang in a loud, shrill soprano, prone now and

then to be flat, and yet, impartially, prone now
and then to be sharp : —

> Thar war two sun-dogs in the red day-dawn,
>   An' the wind war laid — 't war prime fur game.
> I went ter the woods betimes that morn,
>   An' tuk my flint-lock, "Nancy," by name;
>   An' thar I see, in the crotch of a tree,
>   A great big catamount grinnin' at me.
>   A-kee! he! he! An' a-ho! ho! he!
>   A pop-eyed catamount laffin' at me!

And, as Rufe sang, the anger and remonstrance in the owl's demeanor increased every
moment.   For the owl was a vocalist, too!

> Bein' made game of by a brute beastis,
>   War su'thin' I could in no ways allow.
> I jes' spoke up, for my dander hed riz,
>   "Cat — take in the slack o' yer jaw!"
> He bowed his back — Nance sighted him gran',
> Then the blamed old gal jes' flashed in the pan!
>   A-kee! he! he! An' a-ho! ho! he!
>   With a outraged catamount rebukin' of me!

As Rufe finished this with a mighty *cres-
cendo*, he was obliged to pause for breath.
He stared about, gaspily.   The afternoon was
waning.   The mountains close at hand were
a darker green.   The distant ranges had assumed a rosy amethystine tint, like nothing

earthly — like the mountains of a dream, perhaps. The buzzard had alighted in the top of a tree not far down the slope, a tree long ago lightning-scathed, but still rising, gaunt and scarred, above all the forest, and stretching dead stark arms to heaven. Somehow Rufe did not like the looks of it. He was aware of a revulsion of feeling, of the ebbing away of his merry spirit before he saw more.

As he tried to sing : —

> I war the mightiest hunter that ever ye see
> Till that thar catamount tuk arter me! —

his tongue clove suddenly to the roof of his mouth.

He could see something under that tree which no one else could see, not even from the summit of the crags, for the tree was beyond a projecting slope, and out of the range of vision thence.

Rufe could not make out distinctly what the object was, but it was evidently foreign to the place. He possessed the universal human weakness of regarding everything with a personal application. It now seemed strange to him

that he should have come here at all; stranger
still, that he should have mounted this queer
relic of days so long gone by, and thus discovered that peculiar object under the dead tree.
He began to think he had been led here for a
purpose. Now Rufe was not so good a boy as
to be on the continual lookout for rewards of
merit. On the contrary, the day of reckoning
meant with him the day of punishment. He
had heard recounted an unpleasant superstition that when the red sunsets were flaming
round the western mountains, and the valleys
were dark and drear, and the abysses and
gorges gloomed full of witches and weird
spirits, Satan himself might be descried, walk-
ing the crags, and spitting fire, and deporting
himself generally in such a manner as to cause
great apprehension to a small person who could
remember so many sins as Rufe could. His
sins! they trooped up before his mental vision
now, and in a dense convocation crowded the
encompassing wilderness.

Rufe felt that he must not leave this matter
in uncertainty. He must know whether that

strange object under the tree could be intended as a warning to him to cease in time his evil ways — tormenting Towse, pulling Tennessee's hair, shirking the woodpile, and squandering Birt's rifle balls. He even feared this might be a notification that the hour of retribution had already come!

He scuttled off the platform, and began to swing himself from bough to bough. He was nervous and less expert than when he had climbed up the tree. He lost his grip once, and crashed from one branch to another, scratching himself handsomely in the operation. The owl, emboldened by his retreat, flew awkwardly down upon the scaffold, and perched there, its head turned askew, and its great, round eyes fixed solemnly upon him.

Suddenly a wild hoot of derision rent the air; the echoes answered, and all the ravine was filled with the jeering clamor.

"The wust luck in the worl'!" plained poor Rufe, as the ill-omened cry rose again and again. " 'Tain't goin' ter s'prise me none now, ef I gits my neck bruk along o' this resky foolishness in this cur'ous place whar ow*els* watch from the lookout ez dead men hev lef'."

He came down unhurt, however. Then he sidled about a great many times through " the laurel," for he could not muster courage for a direct approach to the strange object he had descried. The owl still watched him, and bobbed its head and hooted after him. When he drew near the lightning - scathed tree, he paused rooted to the spot, gazing in astonishment, his hat on the back of his tow head, his eyes opened wide, one finger inserted in his mouth in silent deprecation.

For there stood a man dressed in black, and with a dark straw hat on his head. He had gray whiskers, and gleaming spectacles of a mildly surprised expression. He smiled kindly when he saw Rufe. Incongruously enough, he had a hammer in his hand. He was going down the ravine, tapping the rocks with it. And Rufe thought he looked for all the world like some over-grown, demented woodpecker.

CHAPTER IV.

As Rufe still stood staring, the old gentleman held out his hand with a cordial gesture.

"Come here, my little man!" he said in a kind voice.

Rufe hesitated. Then he was seized by sudden distrust. Who was this stranger? and why did he call, "Come here!"

Perhaps the fears already uppermost in Rufe's mind influenced his hasty conclusion. He cast a horrified glance upon the old gentleman in black, a garb of suspicious color to the little mountaineer, who had never seen men clad in aught but the brown jeans habitually worn by the hunters of the range. He remembered, too, the words of an old song that chronicled how alluring were the invitations of Satan, and with a frenzied cry he fled frantically through the laurel.

Away and away he dashed, up steep ascents, down sharp declivities, falling twice or thrice in his haste, but hurting his clothes more than himself.

It was not long before he was in sight of home, and Towse met him at the fence. The feeling between these two was often the reverse of cordial, and as Rufe climbed down from rail to rail, his sullen "Lemme 'lone, now!" was answered by sundry snaps at his heels and a low growl. Not that Towse would really have harmed him — fealty to the family forbade that; but in defense of his ears and tail he thought it best to keep fierce possibilities in Rufe's contemplation.

Rufe sat down on the floor of the uninclosed passage between the two rooms, his legs dangling over the sparse sprouts of chickweed and clumps of mullein that grew just beneath, for there were no steps, and Towse bounded up and sat upright close beside him. And as he sought to lean on Towse, the dog sought to lean on him.

They both looked out meditatively at the

dense and sombre wilderness, upon which this little clearing and humble log-cabin were but meagre suggestions of that strong, full-pulsed humanity that has elsewhere subdued nature, and achieved progress, and preëmpted perfection.

Towse soon shut his eyes, and presently he was nodding. Presumably he dreamed, for once he roused himself to snap at a fly, when there was no fly. Rufe, however, was wide awake, and busily canvassing how to account to Birt for the lack of a message from Nate Griggs, for he would not confess how untrustworthy he had proved himself. As he reflected upon this perplexity, he leaned his throbbing head on his hand, and his attitude expressed a downcast spirit.

This chanced to strike his mother's attention as she came to the door. She paused and looked keenly at him.

"Them hoss apples ag'in!" she exclaimed, with the voice of accusation. She had no idea of youthful dejection disconnected with the colic.

Rufe was roused to defend himself. " Hain't teched 'em, now ! " he cried, acrimoniously.

" Waal, sometimes ye air sorter loose-jointed in yer jaw, an' ain't partic'lar what ye say," rejoined his mother, politely. " I 'll waste a leetle yerb-tea on ye, ennyhow."

She started back into the room, and Rufe rose at once. This cruelty should not be practiced upon him, whatever might betide him at the tanyard. He set out at a brisk pace. He had no mind to be long alone in the woods since his strange adventure down the ravine, or he might have hid in the underbrush, as he had often done, until other matters usurped his mother's medicinal intentions.

When Rufe reached the tanyard, Birt was still at work. He turned and looked eagerly at the juvenile ambassador.

" Did Nate gin ye a word fur me ? " he called sonorously, above the clamor of the noisy bark-mill.

" He say he 'll be hyar ter-morrer by sun-up ! " piped out Rufe, in a blatant treble.

A lie seemed less reprehensible when he

was obliged to labor so conscientiously to make it heard.

And then compunction seized him. He sat down by Tennessee on a pile of bark, and took off his old wool hat to mop the cold perspiration that had started on his head and face. He felt sick, and sad, and extremely wicked, — a sorry contrast to Birt, who was so honest and reliable and, as his mother always said, "ez stiddy ez the mounting." Birt was beginning to unharness the mule, for the day's work was at an end.

The dusk had deepened to darkness. The woods were full of gloom. A timorous star palpitated in the sky. In the sudden stillness when the bark-mill ceased its whir, the mountain torrent hard by lifted a mystic chant. The drone of the katydid vibrated in the laurel, and the shrill-voiced cricket chirped. Two of the men were in the shed examining a green hide by the light of a perforated tin lantern, that seemed to spill the rays in glinting white rills. As they flickered across the pile of bark where Rufe and Tennessee were

4

sitting, he noticed how alert Birt looked, how bright his eyes were.

For Birt's hopes were suddenly renewed. He thought that some mischance had detained Nate to-day, and that he would come to-morrow to work at the bark-mill.

The boy's blood tingled at the prospect of being free to seek for treasure down the ravine. He began to feel that he had been too quick to distrust his friend. Perhaps the stipulation that Nate should not go to the ravine until the work commenced was more than he ought to have asked. And perhaps, too, the trespasser was not Nate! The traces of shallow delving might have been left by another hand.

Birt paused reflectively in unharnessing the mule. He stood with the gear in one hand, serious and anxious, in view of the possibility that this discovery was not his alone.

Then he strove to cast aside the thought. He said to himself that he had been hasty in concluding that the slight excavation argued human presence in that lonely spot; a rock dislodged and rolling heavily down the gorge

might have thus scraped into the sand and
gravel; or perhaps some burrowing animal,
prospecting for winter quarters, had begun to
dig a hole under the bowlder.

He was perplexed, despite his plausible reasoning, and he continued silent and preoccupied when he lifted Tennessee to his shoulder
and trudged off homeward, with Rufe at his
heels, and the small boy's conscience following
sturdily in the rear.

That sternly accusing conscience! Rufe
was dismayed, when he sat with the other
laughing children about the table, to know
that his soul was not merry. Sometimes a
sombre shadow fell upon his face, and once
Birt asked him what was the matter. And
though he laughed more than ever, he felt
it was very hard to be gay without the subtle
essence of mirth. That lie! — it seemed to
grow; before supper was over it was as big
as the warping-bars, and when they all sat in
a semicircle in the open passage, Rufe felt that
his conscience was the most prominent mem-
ber of the party. The young moon sank; the

night waxed darker still; the woods murmured
mysteriously. And he was glad enough at last
to be sent to bed, where after so long a time
sleep found him.

The morrow came in a cloud. The light
lacked the sunshine. The listless air lacked
the wind. Still and sombre, the woods touched
the murky, motionless sky. All the universe
seemed to hold a sullen pause. Time was
afoot — it always is — but Birt might not
know how it sped; no shadows on the spent
tan this dark day! Over his shoulder he was
forever glancing, hoping that Nate would presently appear from the woods. He saw only
the mists lurking in the laurel; they had au-
tumnal presage and a chill presence. He but-
toned his coat about him, and the old mule
sneezed as he jogged round the bark-mill.

Jubal Perkins and a crony stood smoking
much of the time to-day in the door of the
house, looking idly out upon the brown stretch
of spent bark, and the gray, weather-beaten
sheds, and the dun sky, and the shadowy, mist-
veiled woods. The tanner was a tall, muscular

man, clad in brown jeans, and with boots of a
fair grade of leather drawn high over his trousers. As he often remarked, "The tanyard
owes *me* good foot-gear — ef the rest o' the
mounting hev ter go barefoot." The expression of his face was somewhat masked by a
heavy grizzled beard, but from beneath the
wide brim of his hat his eyes peered out with
a jocose twinkle. His mouth seemed chiefly
useful as a receptacle for his pipe-stem, for he
spoke through his nose. His voice was strident on the air, since he included in the conversation a workman in the shed, who was
scraping with a two-handled knife a hide
spread on a wooden horse. This man, whose
name was Andrew Byers, glanced up now and
then, elevating a pair of shaggy eyebrows, and
settled the affairs of the nation with diligence
and despatch, little hindered by his labors or
the distance.

Birt took no heed of the loud drawling talk.
In moody silence he drove the mule around
and around the bark-mill. The patient old
animal, being in no danger of losing his way,

closed his eyes drowsily as he trudged, making the best of it.

"I 'll git ez mild-mannered an' meek-hearted ez this hyar old beastis, some day, ef things keep on ez disapp'intin' ez they hev been lately," thought Birt, miserably. "They do say ez even he used ter be a turrible kicker."

Noon came and went, and still the mists hung in the forest closely engirdling the little clearing. The roofs glistened with moisture, and the eaves dripped. A crow was cawing somewhere. Birt had paused to let the mule rest, and the raucous sound caused him to turn his head. His heart gave a bound when he saw that on the other side of the fence the underbrush was astir along the path which wound through the woods to the tanyard. Somebody was coming; he hoped even yet that it might be Nate. He eagerly watched the rustling boughs. The crow had flown, but he heard as he waited a faint "caw! caw!" in the misty distance. Whoever the newcomer might be, he certainly loitered. At last the leaves parted, and revealed — Rufe.

Birt's first sensation was renewed disappointment. Then he was disposed to investigate the mystery of Nate's non-appearance.

"Hello, Rufe!" he called out, as soon as the small boy was inside the tanyard, "be you-uns *sure* ez Nate said he'd come over by sun-up?"

Rufe halted and gazed about him, endeavoring to conjure an expression of surprise into his freckled face. He even opened his mouth to exhibit astonishment — exhibiting chiefly that equivocal tongue, and a large assortment of jagged squirrel teeth.

"Hain't Nate come yit?" he ventured.

The tanner suddenly put into the conversation.

"War it Nate Griggs ez ye war aimin' ter trade with ter take yer place wunst in a while in the tanyard?"

Birt assented. "An' he 'lowed he'd be hyar ter-day by sun-up. Rufe brung that word from him yestiddy."

Rufe's conscience had given him a recess, during which he had consumed several horse-apples in considerable complacence and a total disregard of "yerb tea." He had climbed a tree, and sampled a green persimmon, and he endured with fortitude the pucker in his mouth, since it enabled him to make such faces at Towse as caused the dog to snap and growl in a frenzy of surprised indignation. He had fashioned a corn-stalk fiddle — that instrument so dear to rural children! — and he had been sawing away on it to his own satisfaction and Tennessee's unbounded admiration for the last half-hour. He had forgotten that pursuing conscience till it seized upon him again in the tanyard.

"Oh, Birt," he quavered out, suddenly, " I hain't laid eyes on Nate."

Birt exclaimed indignantly, and Jubal Perkins laughed.

" I seen sech a cur'ous lookin' man, down in the ravine by the lick, ez it sot me all catawampus !" continued Rufe.

As he told of his defection, and the falsehood with which he had accounted for it, Jubal Perkins came to a sudden decision.

"Git on that thar mule, Birt, an' ride over ter Nate's, an' find out what ails him, ef so be ye hanker ter know. I don't want nobody workin' in this hyar tanyard ez looks ez mournful ez ye do — like ez ef ye hed been buried an' dug up. But hurry back, 'kase there ain't enough bark ground yit, an' I hev got other turns o' work I want ye ter do besides 'fore dark."

"War that Satan?" asked Rufe abruptly.

"Whar?" exclaimed Birt, startled, and glancing hastily over his shoulder.

"Down yander by the lick," plained Rufe.

"Naw!" said Birt, scornfully, "an' nuthin' like Satan, I'll be bound!"

He was, however, uneasy to hear of any man down the ravine in the neighborhood of his hidden treasure, but he could not now question Rufe, for Jube Perkins, with mock severity, was taking the small boy to account.

Byers was looking on, the knife idle in his hands, and his lips distended with a wide grin in the anticipation of getting some fun out of Rufe.

"Look-a-hyar, bub," said Jubal Perkins, with both hands in his pockets and glaring down solemnly at Rufe; "ef ever I ketches ye goin' of yerrands no better' n that ag'in, I 'm a-goin' ter — *tan* that thar hide o' yourn."

Rufe gazed up deprecatingly, his eyes widening at the prospect. Byers broke into a horse laugh.

"We 've been wantin' some leetle varmints fur tanning ennyhow," he said. "Ye 'll feel mighty queer when ye stand out thar on the spent tan, with jes' yer meat on yer bones, an 'look up an' see yer skin a-hangin' alongside o' the t 'other calves, an' sech — that ye will!"

"An' all the mounting folks will be remarkin' on it, too," said Perkins. Which no doubt they would have done with a lively interest.

"I reckon," said Byers, looking speculatively at Rufe, "ez 't would take a right smart time fur ye ter git tough enough ter go 'bout in respect'ble society ag'in. 'T would hurt ye mightily, I 'm thinkin'. Ef I war you-uns,

I 'd be powerful partic'lar ter keep inside o' sech an accommodatin'-lookin' little hide ez yourn be fur tanning."

Rufe's countenance was distorted. He seemed about to tune up and whimper. " An' ef I war you-uns, Andy Byers, I 'd find su'- thin' better ter do 'n ter bait an' badger a crit- ter the size o' Rufe! " exclaimed Birt angrily.

"That thar boy 's 'bout right, too! " said the man who had hitherto been standing silent in the door.

" Waal, leave Rufe be, Jubal! " said Byers, laughing. " *Ye* started the fun."

" Leave him be, yerself," retorted the tanner.

When Birt mounted the mule, and rode out of the yard, he glanced back and saw that Rufe had approached the shed; judging by his gestures, he was asking a variety of ques- tions touching the art of tanning, to which Byers amicably responded.

The mists were shifting as Birt went on and on. He heard the acorns dropping from the chestnut-oaks — sign that the wind was awake in the woods. Like a glittering, polished

blade, at last a slanting sunbeam fell. It split
the gloom, and a radiant afternoon seemed to
emerge. The moist leaves shone ; far down
the aisles of the woods the fugitive mists, in
elusive dryadic suggestions, chased each other
into the distance. Although the song-birds
were all silent, there was a chirping somewhere
— cheerful sound! He had almost reached
his destination when a sudden rustling in the
undergrowth by the roadside caused him to
turn and glance back.

Two or three shoats lifted their heads and
were gazing at him with surprise, and a certain disfavor, as if they did not quite like his
looks. A bevy of barefooted, tow-headed children were making mud pies in a marshy dip
close by. An ancient hound, that had re-
nounced the chase and assumed in his old age
the office of tutor, seemed to preside with dig-
nity and judgment. He, too, had descried the
approach of the stranger. He growled, but
made no other demonstration.

" Whar 's Nate ? " Birt called out, for these
were the children of Nate's eldest brother.

For a moment there was no reply. Then
the smallest of the small boys shrilly piped
out, "He hev gone away! — him an' gran'-
dad's claybank mare."

Another unexpected development! "When
will he come back?"

"Ain't goin' ter come back fur two weeks."

"Whar 'bouts hev he gone?" asked Birt
amazed.

"Dunno," responded the same little fellow.

"When did he set out?"

There was a meditative pause. Then ensued a jumbled bickering. The small boys,
the shoats, and the hound seemed to consult
together in the endeavor to distinguish "day
'fore yestiddy" from "las' week." The
united intellect of the party was inadequate.

"Dunno!" the mite of a spokesman at last
admitted.

Birt rode on rapidly once more, leaving this
choice syndicate settling down again to the
mud pies.

The woods gave way presently and revealed,
close to a precipice, Nate's home. The log

house with its chimney of clay and sticks, the
barn of ruder guise, the fodder-stack, the ash-
hopper, and the rail fence were all imposed in
high relief against the crimson west and the
purpling ranges in the distance. The little
cabin was quite alone in the world. No other
house, no field, no clearing, was visible in all
the vast expanse of mountains and valleys
which it overlooked. The great panorama of
nature seemed to be unrolled for it only. The
seasons passed in review before it. The moon
rose, waxing or waning, as if for its behoof.
The sun conserved for it a splendid state.

But the skies above it had sterner moods,
— sometimes lightnings veined the familiar
clouds ; winds rioted about it ; the thunder
spoke close at hand. And then it was that
Mrs. Griggs lamented her husband's course in
" raisin' the house hyar so nigh the bluffs ez
ef it war an' aigle's nest," and forgot that she
had ever accounted herself " sifflicated " when
distant from the airy cliffs.

She stood in the doorway now, her arms
akimbo — an attitude that makes a woman of

a certain stamp seem more masterful than a
man. Her grizzled locks were ornamented by
a cotton cap with a wide and impressive ruffle,
which, swaying and nodding, served to empha-
size her remarks. She was conferring in a
loud drawl with her husband, who had let
down the bars to admit his horse, laden with
a newly killed deer. Her manner would seem
to imply that she, and not he, had slain the
animal.

" Toler'ble fat," she commented with grave
self-complacence. " He 'minds me sorter o'
that thar tremenjious buck we hed las' Sep-
tember. *He* war the fattes' buck I ever see.
Take off his hide right straight."

The big cap-ruffle flapped didactically.

" Lor'-a - massy, woman! " vociferated the
testy old man ; " ain't I a-goin' ter ? Ter hear
ye a-jowin', a-body would think I had never
shot nothin' likelier'n a yaller-hammer sence
I been born. S'pos'n ye jes' takes ter goin'
a-huntin', an' skinnin' deer, an' cuttin' wood,
an' doin' my work ginerally. Pears-like ye
think ye knows mo' 'bout'n my work 'n I does.
An' I 'll bide hyar at the house."

Mrs. Griggs nodded her head capably, in nowise dismayed. " I dunno but that plan would work mighty well," she said.

This conjugal colloquy terminated as she glanced up and saw Birt.

" Why, thar 's young Dicey a - hint ye. Howdy Birt ! 'Light an' hitch ! "

" Naw 'm," rejoined Birt, as he rode into the enclosure and close up to the doorstep. " I hain't got time ter 'light." Then precipitately opening the subject of his mission. " I kem over hyar ter see Nate. Whar hev he disappeared ter ? "

" Waal, now, that 's jes' what I 'd like ter know," she replied, her face eloquent with baffled curiosity. " He jes' borried his dad's claybank mare, an' sot out, an' never 'lowed whar he war bound fur. Nate hev turned twenty-one year old," she continued, " an' he 'lows he air a man growed, an' obligated ter obey nobody but hisself. From the headin' way that he kerries on hyar, a-body would s'pose he air older 'n the Cumberland Mountings ! But he hev turned twenty-one — that 's a fac' — an' he voted at the las' election."

"WAAL, NOW, THAT'S JES' WHAT I'D LIKE TER KNOW." See page 64.

(With how much discretion it need not now be inquired.)

" I knows that air true," said Birt, who had wistfully admired this feat of his senior.

" Waal — Nate don't set much store by votin'," rejoined Mrs. Griggs. " Nate, he say, the greatest privilege his kentry kin confer on him is ter make it capital punishment fur wimmen ter ax him questions ! — Which I hev done," she admitted stoutly.

And the ruffle on her cap did not deny it.

" Nate air twenty-one," she reiterated. " An' I s'pose he 'lows ez I hev no call nowadays ter be his mother."

" Hain't ye got no guess whar he be gone ? " asked Birt, dismayed by this strange new complication.

" Waal, I hev been studyin' it out ez Nate mought hev rid ter Parch Corn, whar his great - uncle, Joshua Peters, lives — him that merried my aunt, Melissy Baker, ez war a widder then, though born a Scruggs. An' then, ag'in, Nate *mought* hev tuk it inter his head ter go ter the Cross-roads, a-courtin' a gal

5

thar ez he hev been talkin' about powerful,
lately. But they tells me," Mrs. Griggs ex-
postulated, as it were, " that them gals at the
Cross-roads is in no way desirable, — specially
this hyar Elviry Mills, ez mighty nigh all the
boys on the mounting hev los' thar wits about,
— what little wits ez they ever hed ter lose,
I mean ter say. But Nate thinks he hev got
a right ter a ch'ice, bein' ez he air turned
twenty-one."

" Did he say when he 'lowed ter come back ? "
Birt asked.

" 'Bout two or three weeks Nate laid off ter
be away ; but whar he hev gone, an' what 's
his yerrand, he let no human know," returned
Mrs. Griggs. " I hev been powerful agger-
vated 'bout this caper o' Nate's. I ain't afeard
he 'll git hisself hurt no ways whilst he be
gone, for Nate is mighty apt ter take keer
o' Nate." She nodded her head convincingly,
and the great ruffle on her cap shook in cor-
roboration. " But I hain't never hed the right
medjure o' respec' out'n Nate, an' his dad
hain't, nuther."

Birt listened vaguely to this account of his friend's filial shortcomings, his absent eyes fixed upon the wide landscape, and his mind busy with the anxious problems of Nate's broken promises.

And the big red ball of the setting sun seemed at last to roll off the plane of the horizon, and it disappeared amidst the fiery emblazonment of clouds with which it had enriched the west. But all the world was not so splendid; midway below the dark purple summits a dun, opaque vapor asserted itself in dreary, aerial suspension. Beneath it he could see a file of cows, homeward bound, along the road that encircled the mountain's base. He heard them low, and this reminded him that night was near, for all that the zenith was azure, and for all that the west was aglow. And he remembered he had a good many odd jobs to do before dark. And so he turned his face homeward.

CHAPTER V.

BIRT had always been held in high esteem by the men at the tanyard. Suddenly, however, the feeling toward him cooled. He remembered afterward, although at the time he was too absorbed to fully appreciate it, that this change began one day shortly after he had learned of Nate's departure. As he went mechanically about his work, he was pondering futilely upon his friend's mysterious journey, and his tantalizing hopes lying untried in the depths of the ravine. He hardly noticed the conversation of the men until something was said that touched upon the wish nearest his heart.

"I war studyin' 'bout lettin' Birt hev a day off," said the tanner. "An' ye 'll bide hyar."

"Naw, Jube — naw!" Andy Byers replied with stalwart independence to his employer.

"I hev laid off ter attend. Ef ye want enny-body ter bide with the tanyard, an' keer fur this hyar pit, ye kin do it yerse'f, or else Birt kin. *I* hev laid off ter attend."

Andy Byers was a man of moods. His shaggy eyebrows to-day overshadowed eyes sombre and austere. He seemed, if possible, a little slower than was his wont. He bore himself with a sour solemnity, and he was at once irritable and dejected.

"Shucks, Andy! ye knows ye ain't no kin sca'cely ter the old woman; ye could n't count out how ye air kin ter her ter. save yer life. Now, *I*'m obleeged ter attend."

It so happened that the tanner's great-aunt was distantly related to Andy Byers. Being ill, and an extremely old woman, she was sup-posed to be lying at the point of death, and her kindred had been summoned to hear her last words.

"I hed 'lowed ter gin Birt a day off, 'kase I hev got ter hev the mule in the wagon, an' he can't grind bark. I *promised* Birt a day off," the tanner continued.

"That thar's twixt ye an' Birt. I hain't got no call ter meddle," said the obdurate Byers. "Ye kin bide with the tanyard an' finish this job yerse'f, ef so minded. *I*'m goin' ter attend."

"I reckon half the kentry-side will be thar, an' *I* wants ter see the folks," said Jubal Perkins, cheerfully.

"Then Birt will hev ter bide with the tanyard, an' finish this job. It don't lie with me ter gin him a day off. I don't keer ef he never gits a day off," said Byers.

This was an unnecessarily unkind speech, and Birt's anger flamed out.

"Ef we-uns war of a size, Andy Byers," he said, hotly, "I 'd make ye divide work a leetle more ekal than ye does."

Andy Byers dropped the hide in his hands, and looked steadily across the pit at Birt, as if he were taking the boy's measure.

"Ye mean ter say ef ye hed the bone an' muscle ye 'd knock me down, do ye?" he sneered. "Waal, I 'll take the will fur the deed. I 'll hold the grudge agin ye, jes' the same."

They were all three busied about the pit.
The hides had been taken out, and stratified
anew, with layers of fresh tan, reversing the
original order, — those that had been at the bot-
tom now being placed at the top. The operation was almost complete before Jubal Perkins
received the news of his relative's precarious
condition. He had no doubt that Birt was
able to finish it properly, and the boy's consci-
entious habit of doing his best served to make
the tanner's mind quite easy. As to the day
off, he was glad to have that question settled
by a quarrel between his employees, thus re-
lieving him of responsibility.

Birt's wrath was always evanescent, and he
was sorry a moment afterward for what he
had said. Andy Byers exchanged no more
words with him, and skillfully combined a curt
and crusty manner toward him with an aspect
of contemplative dreariness. Occasionally, as
they paused to rest, Byers would sigh deeply.

"A mighty good old woman, Mrs. Price
war." He spoke as if she were already dead.
"A mighty good old woman, though small-
sized."

" A little of her went a long way. She war eighty-four year old, an' kep' a sharp tongue in her head ter the las'," rejoined the tanner, adopting in turn the past tense.

Rufe listened with startled interest. Now and then he cocked up his speculative eyes, and gazed fixedly into the preternaturally solemn face of Byers, who reiterated, " A good old woman, though small-sized."

With this unaccustomed absorption Rufe's accomplishment of getting under-foot became pronounced. The tanner jostled him more than once, Birt stumbled against his toes, and Byers, suddenly turning, ran quite over him. Rufe had not far to fall, but Byers was a tall man. His arms swayed like the sails of a windmill in the effort to recover his balance. He was in danger of toppling into the pit, and in fact only caught himself on his knees at its verge.

" Ye torment! " he roared angrily, as he struggled to his feet. " G'way from hyar, or I 'll skeer ye out'n yer wits ! "

The small boy ruefully gathered his mem-

bers together, and after the men had started
on their journey he sat down on a pile of wood
hard by to give Birt his opinion of Andy
Byers.

"He air a toler'ble mean man, ain't he,
Birt?"

But Birt said he had no mind to talk about
Andy Byers.

" *Skeer me!* " exclaimed Rufe, doughtily.
" It takes a heap ter skeer *Me!* "

He got up presently, and going into the
shed began to examine the tools of the trade
which were lying there. He had the two-handled knife, with which he was about to try his
skill on a hide that was stretched over the
beam of the wooden horse, when Birt glanced
up and came hastily to the rescue. Rufe was
disposed to further investigate the appliances
of the tanyard left defenseless at his mercy,
but at last Birt prevailed on him to go home
and play with Tennessee, and was glad enough
to see his tow-head, with his old hat perched
precariously on it, bobbing up and down
among the low bushes, as he wended his way
along the path through the woods.

The hides had•all been replaced between layers of fresh tan before the men left, and Birt had only to fill up the space above with a thicker layer, ten or fifteen inches deep, and put the boards securely across the top of the pit, with heavy stones upon them to weight them down. But this kept him busy all the rest of the afternoon.

Rufe was pretty busy too. When he came in sight of home Tennessee was the first object visible in the open passage. The sunshine slanted through it under the dusky roof, and the shadows of the chestnut-oak, hard by, dappled the floor. Lying there was an old Mexican saddle, for which there was no use since the horse had died. Tennessee was mounted upon it, the reins in her hands, the headstall and bit poised on the peaked pommel. She jounced back and forth, and the skirts of the saddle flapped and the stirrups clanked on the floor, and the absorbed eyes of the little mountaineer were fixed on space.

Away and away she cantered on some splendid imaginary palfrey, through scenes where

conjecture fails to follow her : a land, doubtless, where all the winds blow fair, and spark-
ling waters run, and jeopardy delights, and
fancy's license prevails — all very different,
you may be sure, from the facts, an old saddle
on a puncheon floor, and a little black-eyed
mountaineer.

How far Tennessee journeyed, and how long
she was gone, it is impossible to say. She
halted suddenly when her attention was attracted to a phenomenon within one of the
rooms.

The door was ajar and the solitary Rufe was
visible in the dusky vista. He stood before a
large wooden chest. He had lifted the lid,
and kept it up by resting it upon his head,
bent forward for the purpose, while he rum-
maged the contents with vandal hands.

Tennessee stared at him, with indignant surprise gathering in her widening eyes.

Now that chest contained, besides a meagre
store of quilts and comforts, her own and her
mother's clothes, the fewer garments of the
boys of the family being alternately suspended

on the clothes-line and their own frames. She resented the sacrilege of Rufe's invasion of that chest. She turned on the saddle and looked around with an air of appeal. Her mother, however, was down the hill beside the spring, busy boiling soap, and quite out of hearing. Tennessee gazed vaguely for a moment at the great kettle with the red and yellow flames curling around it, and her mother's figure hovering over it. Then she looked back at Rufe.

He continued industriously churning up the contents of the chest, the lid still poised upon that head that served so many other useful purposes — for the gymnastic exhibition involved in standing on it; for his extraordinary mental processes; for a lodgment for his old wool hat, and a field for his crop of flaxen hair.

All the instinct of the proprietor was roused within Tennessee. She found her voice, a hoarse, infantile wheeze.

"Tum out'n chist!" she exclaimed, gutturally. "Tum out'n chist!"

Rufe turned his tow-head slowly, that he might not disturb the poise of the lid of the chest resting upon it. He fixed a solemn stare on Tennessee, and drawing one hand from the depths of the chest, he silently shook his fist. And then he resumed his researches.

Tennessee, alarmed by this impressive demonstration, dismounted hastily from the saddle as soon as his threatening gaze was withdrawn. She tangled her feet in the stirrups and her hands in the reins, and lost more time in scrambling off the floor of the passage and down upon the ground; but at last she was fairly on her way to the spring to convey an account to her mother of the outlaw in the chest. In fact, she was not far from the scene of the soap-boiling when she heard her name shouted in stentorian tones, and pausing to look back, she saw Rufe gleefully capering about in the passage, the headstall on his own head, the bit hanging on his breast, and the reins dangling at his heels.

Now this beguilement the little girl could never withstand, and indeed few people ever had the opportunity to drive so frisky and high-spirited a horse as Rufe was when he consented to assume the bit and bridle. He was rarely so accommodating, as he preferred the role of driver, with what he called "a pop-lashee !" at command. She forgot her tell-tale mission. She turned with a gurgle of delight and began to toddle up the hill again. And presently Mrs. Dicey, glancing toward the house, saw them playing together in great amity, and rejoiced that they gave her so little trouble.

They were still at it when Birt came home, but then Tennessee was tired of driving,.and he let her go with him to the wood-pile and sit on a log while he swung the axe. No one took special notice of Rufe's movements in the interval before supper. He disappeared for a time, but when the circle gathered around the table he was in his place and by no means a non-combatant in the general onslaught on the corn-dodgers. Afterward he came out in the passage and sat quietly among the others.

The freshened air was fragrant, and how

the crickets were chirring in the grass! On every spear the dew was a-glimmer, for a lustrous moon shone from the sky. Somehow, despite the long roads of light that this splendid pioneer blazed out in the wilderness, it seemed only to reveal the loneliness of the forests, and to give new meaning to the solemnity of the shadows. The heart was astir with some responsive thrill that jarred vaguely, and was pain. Yet the night had its melancholy fascination, and they were all awake later than usual. When at last the doors were barred, and the house grew still, and even the vigilant Towse had ceased to bay and had lodged himself under the floor of the passage, the moon still shone in isolated effulgence, for the faint stars faded before it.

The knowledge that in all the vast stretch of mountain fastnesses he was the only human creature that beheld it, as it majestically crossed the meridian, gave Andy Byers a forlorn feeling, while tramping along homeward. He had made the journey afoot, some eight miles down the valley, and was later far in re-

turning than others who had heeded the summons of the sick woman. For she still lay
in the same critical condition, and his mind
was full of dismal forebodings as he toiled
along the road on the mountain's brow. The
dark woods were veined with shimmering silver. The mists, hovering here and there,
showed now a blue and now an amber gleam
as the moon's rays conjured them. On one
side of the road an oak tree had been uptorn
in a wind-storm ; the roots, carrying a great
mass of earth with them, were thrust high in
the air, while the bole and leafless branches
lay prone along the ground. This served as a
break in the density of the forest, and the
white moonshine possessed the vacant space.

As he glanced in that direction his heart
gave a great bound, then seemed suddenly to
stand still. There, close to the verge of the
road, as if she had stepped aside to let him
pass, was the figure of an old woman — a small-
sized woman, tremulous and bent. It looked
like old Mrs. Price ! As he paused amazed,
with starting eyes and failing limbs, the wind

fluttered her shawl and her ample sunbonnet. This shielded her face and he could not see her features. Her head seemed to turn toward him. The next instant it nodded at him familiarly.

To the superstitious mountaineer this suggested that the old woman had died since he had left her house, and here was her ghost already vagrant in the woods!

The foolish fellow did not wait to put this fancy to the test. With a piercing cry he sprang past, and fled like a frightened deer through the wilderness homeward.

In his own house he hardly felt more secure. He could not rest — he could not sleep. He stirred the embers with a trembling hand, and sat shivering over them. His wife, willing enough to believe in " harnts " [1] as appearing to other people, was disposed to repudiate them when they presumed to offer their dubious association to members of her own family circle.

" Dell-law ! " she exclaimed scornfully. " I

[1] Ghosts.

6

say harnt! Old Mrs. Price, though spry ter
the las', war so proud o' her age an' her ail-
ments that she would n't hev nobody see her
walk a step, or stand on her feet, fur nuthin'. Her darter-in-law tole me ez the only
way ter find out how nimble she really be
war ter box one o' her gran'chill'n, an' then
she'd bounce out'n her cheer, an' jounce
round the room after thar daddy or mammy,
whichever hed boxed the chill'n. That fur-
saken couple always hed ter drag thar chill'n
out in the woods, out'n earshot of the house,
ter whip 'em, an' then threat 'em ef they
dare let thar granny know they hed been
struck. But elsewise she hed ter be lifted
from her bed ter her cheer by the h'a'th. She
would n't hev *her* sperit seen a-walkin' way up
hyar a-top o' the mounting, like enny healthy
harnt, fur nuthin' in this worl'. Whatever
't war, 't warn't *her*. An' I reckon ef the truth
war knowed, 't warn't nuthin' at all — forg,
mebbe."

This stalwart reasoning served to steady his
nerves a little. And when the moon went

"THE FIGURE OF A LITTLE, BENT OLD WOMAN—NAY, IN THE BRIGHTENING DAWN, A BUSH." See page 83.

down and the day was slowly breaking, he took
his way, with a vacillating intention and many
a chilling doubt, along the winding road to
the scene of his fright.

It was not yet time by a good hour or more
to go to work, and nothing was stirring. A
wan light was on the landscape when he came
in sight of the great tree prone upon the
ground. And there, close to the edge of the
road, as if she had stepped aside to let him
pass, was the figure of a little, bent old woman
— nay, in the brightening dawn, a bush — a
blackberry bush, clad in a blue-checked apron,
a red plaid shawl, and with a neat sunbonnet
nodding on its topmost spray.

His first emotion was intense relief. Then
he stood staring at the bush in rising indignation. This sandy by-way of a road led only
to his own house, and this image of a small
and bent old woman had doubtless been devised, to terrify him, by some one who knew
of his mission, and that he could not return
except by this route.

Only for a moment did he feel uncertain

as to the ghost-maker's identity. There was
something singularly familiar to him in the
plaid of the shawl — even in the appearance
of the bonnet, although it was now limp and
damp. He saw it at "meet'n" whenever the
circuit rider preached, and he presently recognized it. This was Mrs. Dicey's bonnet!

His face hardened. He set his teeth together. An angry flush flared to the roots of
his hair.

Not that he suspected the widow of having
set this trap to frighten him. He was not
learned, nor versed in feminine idiosyncrasies,
but it does not require much wisdom to know
that on no account whatever does a woman's
best bonnet stay out all night in the dew, in-
tentionally. The presence of her bonnet
proved the widow's *alibi*.

Like a flash he remembered Birt's anger
the previous day. "Told me he'd make me
divide work mo' ekal, an' ez good ez said he'd
knock me down ef he could. An' I told him
I'd hold the grudge agin him jes' the same —
an' I will!"

He felt sure that it was Birt who had thus taken revenge, because he was kept at work while his fellow-laborer was free to go.

Byers thought the boy would presently come to take the garments home, and conceal his share in the matter, before any one else would be likely to stir abroad.

"An' I 'll hide close by with a good big hickory stick, an' I 'll gin him a larrupin' ez he won't furgit in a month o' Sundays," he resolved, angrily.

He opened his clasp-knife, and walked slowly into the woods, looking about for a choice hickory sprout. He did not at once find one of a size that he considered appropriate to the magnitude of Birt's wickedness, and he went further perhaps than he realized, and stayed longer.

He had a smile of stern satisfaction on his face when he was lopping off the leaves and twigs of a specimen admirably adapted for vengeance. He was stealthy in returning, keeping behind the trees, and slipping softly from bole to bole. At last, as the winding road was once more in view, he crouched down behind the roots of the great fallen oak.

"I don't want him ter git a glimge of me, an' skeer him off afore I kin lay a-holt on him," he said.

He intended to keep the neighboring bush under close watch, and through the interlacing roots he peered out furtively at it. His eyes distended and he hastily rose from his hiding-place.

The blackberry bush was swaying in the wind, clothed only in its own scant and rusty leaves. A wren perched on a spray, chirped cheerful matins.

CHAPTER VI.

HIS scheme was thwarted. The boy had come and gone in his absence, all unaware of his proximity and the impending punishment so narrowly escaped.

But when Andy Byers reached the tanyard and went to work, he said nothing to Birt. He did not even allude to the counterfeit apparition in the woods, although Mrs. Price's probable recovery was more than once under discussion among the men who came and went, — indeed, she lived many years thereafter, to defend her lucky grandchildren against every device of discipline. Byers had given heed to more crafty counsels. On the whole he was now glad that he had not had the opportunity to make Birt and the hickory sprout acquainted with each other. This would be an acknowledgment that he had been terrified by the manufactured ghost, and he preferred foregoing open revenge to encountering the jocose tanner's ridicule, and the gibes that would circulate at his expense throughout the country-side. But he cherished the grievance, and he resolved that Birt should rue it. He had expected that Birt would boast of having frightened him. He intended to admit that he had been a trifle startled, and in treating the matter thus lightly he hoped it would seem that the apparition was a failure.

However, day by day passed and nothing was said. The ghost vanished as mysteriously as it had come. Only Mrs. Dicey, taking her bonnet and apron and shawl from the chest, was amazed at the extraordinary manner in which they were folded and at their limp condition, and when she found a bunch of cockle-burs in the worsted fringes of the shawl she declared that witches must have had it, for she had not worn it since early in April when there were no cockle-burs. She forthwith nailed a horseshoe on the door to keep the witches out, and she never liked the shawl so well after she had projected a mental picture of a lady wearing it, riding on a broomstick, and sporting also a long peaked nose.

Birt hardly noticed the crusty and ungracious conduct of Andy Byers toward him. He worked on doggedly, scheming all the time to get off from the tanyard, and wondering again and again why Nate had gone, and where, and when he would return.

One day — a gray day it was and threatening rain — as he came suddenly out of the shed, he saw a boy at the bars. It was Nate Griggs! No; only for a moment he thought this was Nate. But this fellow's eyes were not so close together; his hair was less sandy; there were no facial indications of extreme slyness. It was only Nathan's humble likeness, his younger brother, Timothy.

He had Nate's coat thrown over his arm, and he shouldered his brother's rifle.

Tim came slouching slowly into the tanyard, a good-natured grin on his face. He paused only to knock Rufe's hat over his eyes,

as the small boy stood in front of the low-
spirited mule, both hands busy with the animal's mouth, striving to open his jaws to judge
by his teeth how old he might be.

"The critter 'll bite ye, Rufe!" Birt exclaimed, for as Rufe stooped to pick up his
hat the mule showed some curiosity in his
turn, and was snuffling at Rufe's hay-colored
hair.

Rufe readjusted his head-gear, and ceasing
his impolite researches into the mule's age,
came up to the other two boys. Tim had
paused by the shed, and leaning upon the rifle,
began to talk.

"I war a-passin' by, an' I thought I 'd drap
in on ye."

"Hev you-uns hearn from Nate since he
hev been gone away?" demanded Birt anxiously.

"He hev come home," responded Tim.

"When did he git home?" Birt asked with
increasing suspicion.

"Las' week," said Tim carelessly.

Another problem! Why had Nate not com-

municated with his partner about their proposed work? It seemed a special avoidance.

"I onderstood ez how he aimed ter bide
away longer," Birt remarked.

"He did count on stayin' longer," said Tim,
"but he rid night an' day ter git hyar sooner.
It 'pears like ter me he war in sech a hurry so
ez ter start *me* ter work, and nuthin' else in
this worl'. I owe Nate a debt, ye see, an' I
hev ter work it out. I hev been so onlucky
ez I could n't make out ter pay him nohow in
the worl'. Ye see, I traded with Nate fur a
shoat, an' the spiteful beastis sneaked out'n
my pen, an' went rootin' round the aidge o'
the clearin', an' war toted off bodaciously by
a bar ez war a-prowlin' round thar. An' I got
no good o' that thar shoat, 'kase the bar hed
him, but I hed to pay fur him all the same.
An' dad gin his cornsent ter Nate ter let me
work a month an' better fur him, ter pay out'n
debt fur the shoat."

"What work be you-uns goin' ter do?"
Birt had a strong impression, amounting to a
conviction, that there was something behind
all this, which he was slowly approaching.

"Why," said Tim, in surprise, " hain't ye hearn bout'n Nate's new land what he hev jes' got 'entered' ez he calls it? He hev got a grant fur it from the land-office down yander in Sparty, whar he hev been."

" New land — '*entered!*' " faltered Birt.

Tim nodded. "Nate fund a trac' o' land a-layin' ter suit his mind what b'longed ter nobody but the State — vacant land, ye see — an' so he went ter the 'entry-taker,' they calls him, an' gits it 'entered,' an' the surveyor kem an' medjured it, an' then Nate got a grant fur it, an' now it air his'n. The Gov'nor o' the State hev sot his name ter that thar grant — the Gov'nor o' Tennessee!" reiterated Tim pridefully. "An' the great seal o' the State!"

"Whar be the land?" gasped Birt, possessed by a dreadful fear.

His face was white, its muscles rigid. Its altered expression could not for an instant have escaped the notice of Timothy's brother Nathan.

"Why, it lays bout'n haffen mile off — all

down the ravine nigh that thar salt-lick; but
look-a-hyar, Birt — what ails ye?"

The stunned despair in the white face had
at last arrested his careless attention.

" Don't ye be mindin' of me — I feel sorter
porely an' sick all of a suddint; tell on 'bout
the land an' sech," said Birt.

He sat down on the end of the wood-pile,
and Tim, still leaning on the rifle, recommenced. He was generally much cowed and
kept down by Nate, and was unaccustomed to
respect and consideration. Therefore he felt
a certain gratification in having so attentive a
listener.

" Waal, I never hearn o' this fashion o'
enterin' land like Nate done in all my life
afore; though dad say that's the law in Tennessee, ter git a title ter vacant land ez jes'
b'longs ter the State. Mebbe them air the
ways ez Nate l'arned whilst he war a-hangin'
round the Settlemint so constant, an' forever
talkin' ter the men thar."

Birt's precocity had never let him feel at a
disadvantage with Nate, although his friend

was five years older. Now he began to appreciate that Nate was indeed a man grown, and had become sophisticated in the ways of his primitive world by his association with the other men at the Settlement.

There was a pause. But the luxury of being allowed to talk without contradiction or rebuke presently induced Tim to proceed.

" He war hyar mighty nigh all day long," he said reflectively. "He eat his dinner along of we-uns."

" Who? the Gov'nor o' the State? " exclaimed Birt, astounded.

" Naw, 't war n't *him*," Tim admitted somewhat reluctantly, since Birt seemed disposed to credit "we-uns " with a gubernatorial guest. "It 's the surveyor I 'm talkin' 'bout. Nate hed ter pay him three dollars an' better fur medjurin' the land. He tole Nate ez his land war ez steep an' rocky a spot ez thar war in Tennessee from e-end ter e-end. He axed Nate what ailed him ter hanker ter pay taxes on sech a pack o' bowlders an' bresh. He 'lowed the land war n't wuth a cent an acre."

"What did Nate say?" asked Birt, who hung with feverish interest on every thoughtless word.

"Waal, Nate 'lows ez he hev fund a cur'ous metal on his land; he say it air *gold!*" Tim opened his eyes very wide, and smacked his lips, as if the word tasted good. "He 'lowed ez he need n't hev been in sech a hurry ter enter his land, 'kase the entry-taker told it ter him ez it air the law in Tennessee ez ennybody ez finds a mine or val'able min'ral on vacant land hev got six months extry ter enter the land afore ennybody else kin, an' ef ennybody else wants ter enter it, they hev ter gin the finder o' the mine thirty days' notice."

Tim winked, an impressive demonstration but for the insufficiency of eyelashes : —

"The surveyor he misdoubted, an' 'lowed ez gold hed never been fund in these parts. He said they fund gold in them mountings furder east 'bout twenty odd year ago — in 1831, I believe he said. He 'lowed them mountings hain't got no coal like our'n hev, an' the

Cumberland Mountings hain't got no gold.
An' then in a minit he tuk ter misdoubtin' on
the t'other side o' his mouth. He 'lowed ez
Nate's min'ral *mought* be gold, an' then ag'in
it mought n't."

The essential difference between these two
extremes has afforded scope for vacillation to
more consistent men than the surveyor.

"Thar's the grant right now, in the pocket
o' Nate's coat," said Tim, shifting the garment
on his arm to show a stiff, white folded paper
sticking out of the breast pocket. "I reckon
when he tole me ter tote his gun an' coat
home, he furgot the grant war in his pocket,
'kase he fairly dotes on it, an' won't trest it
out'n his sight."

Nate was in the habit of exacting similar
services from his acquiescent younger brother,
and Tim had his hands full, as he tried to hold
the gun, and turn the coat on his arm. He
finally hung the garment on a peg in the
shed, and shouldered the weapon. Suddenly he
whirled around toward Rufe, who was still
standing by.

" What in the nation air inside o' that thar boy?" he exclaimed. "A chicken, ain't it?"

For a musical treble chirping was heard proceeding apparently from Rufe's pocket. This chicken differed from others that Rufe had put away, in being alive and hearty.

The small boy entered into the conversation with great spirit, to tell that a certain hen which he owned had yesterday come off her nest with fourteen of the spryest deedies that ever stepped. One in especial had so won upon Rufe by its beauty and grace of deportment that he was carrying it about with him, feeding it at close intervals, and housing it in the security of his pocket.

The deedie hardly made a moan. There was no use in remonstrating with Rufe, — everything that came within his eccentric orbit seemed to realize that, — and the deedie was contentedly nestling down in his pocket, apparently resigned to lead the life of a portemonnaie.

Rufe narrated with pardonable pride the fact that, some time before, his great-uncle,

7

Rufus Dicey, had sent to him from the " valley kentry " a present of a pair of game chickens, and that this deedie was from the first egg hatched in the game hen's brood.

But Rufe was not selfish. He offered to give Tim one of the chicks. Now poultry was Tim's weakness. He accepted with more haste than was seemly, and at once asked for the deedie in the small boy's pocket. Rufe, however, refused to part from the chick of his adoption, and presently Tim, with the gun on his shoulder, left the tanyard in company with Rufe, to look over the brood of game chicks, and make a selection from among them.

Birt hardly noticed what they did or said. Every faculty was absorbed in considering the wily game which his false friend had played so successfully. It was all plain enough now. The fruit of his discovery would be plucked by other hands. There was to be no division of the profits. Nate Griggs had coveted the whole. His craft had secured it for himself alone. He had the legal title to the land, the mine — all ! There seemed absolutely no vul-

nerable point in his scheme. With suddenly
sharpened perceptions, Birt realized that if he
should now claim the discovery and the conse-
quent right of thirty days' notice of Nate's
intention, by virtue of the priority of entering
land accorded by the statute to the finder of
a mine or valuable mineral, it would be considered a groundless boast, actuated by envy
and jealousy. He had told no one but Nate
of his discovery — and would not Nate now
deny it!

However, one thing in the future was certain, — Nathan Griggs should not escape altogether scathless. For a long time Birt sat
motionless, revolving vengeful purposes in his
mind. Every moment he grew more bitter, as
he reflected upon his wrecked scheme, his wonderful fatuity, and the double dealing of his
chosen coadjutor. But he would get even with
Nate Griggs yet; he promised himself that, —
he would get even!

At last the falling darkness warned him
home. When he rose his limbs trembled, his
head was in a whirl, and the familiar scene

swayed, strange and distorted, before him. He steadied himself after a moment, finished the odd jobs he had left undone, and presently was trudging homeward.

A heavy black cloud overhung the woods; an expectant stillness brooded upon the sultry world; an angry storm was in the air. The first vivid flash and simultaneous peal burst from the sky as he reached the passage between the two rooms.

"Ye air powerful perlite ter come a-steppin' home jes' at supper-time," said his mother advancing to meet him. "Ye lef' no wood hyar, an' ye said ye would borry the mule, an' come home early a-purpose to haul some. An' me hyar with nuthin' to cook supper with but sech chips an' blocks an' bresh ez I could pick up off'n the groun'."

Birt's troubles had crowded out the recollection of this domestic duty.

"I clean furgot," he admitted, penitently.

Then he asked suddenly, "An' whar war Rufe, an' Pete, an' Joe, ez *ye* hed ter go ter pickin' up of chips an' sech off'n the groun'?"

He turned toward the group of small boys. "Air you-uns all disabled somehows, ez ye can't pick up chips an' bresh an' sech?" he said. "An' ef ye air, why n't ye go ter the tanyard arter me?"

"They war all off in the woods, a-lookin' arter Rufe's trap ez ye sot fur squir'ls," Mrs. Dicey explained. "It hed one in it, an' I cooked it fur supper."

Birt said that he could go out early with his axe and cut enough wood for breakfast to-morrow, and then he fell silent. Once or twice his preoccupied demeanor called forth comment.

"Why n't ye eat some o' the squir'l, Birt?" his mother asked at the supper table. "Pearslike ter me ez it air cooked toler'ble tasty."

Birt could not eat. He soon rose from the table and resumed his chair by the window, and for half an hour no word passed between them.

The thunder seemed to roll on the very roof of the cabin, and it trembled beneath the heavy fall of the rain. At short intervals a terrible blue light quivered through crevices in the "daubin'" between the logs of the wall, and about the rude shutter which closed the glassless window. Now and then a crash from the forest told of a riven tree. But the storm had no terrors for the inmates of this humble dwelling. Pete and Joe had already gone to bed; Tennessee had fallen asleep while playing on the floor, and Rufe dozed peacefully in his chair. Even Mrs. Dicey nodded as she knitted, the needles sometimes dropping from her nerveless hand.

Birt silently watched the group for a time in the red light of the smouldering fire and the blue flashes from without. At length he softly rose and crept noiselessly to the door; the fastening was the primitive latch with a string attached; it opened without a sound in his cautious handling, and he found himself in the pitchy darkness outside, the wild mountain wind whirling about him, and the rain descending in steady torrents.

He had stumbled only a few steps from the house when he thought he indistinctly heard the door open again. He dreaded his mother's questions, but he stopped and looked back.

He saw nothing. There was no sound save the roar of the wind, the dash of the rain, and the commotion among the branches of the trees.

He went on once more, absorbed in his dreary reflections and the fierce anger that burned in his heart.

" I 'll git even with Nate Griggs," he said, over and again. " I 'll git even with him yit."

CHAPTER VII.

WHEN Birt reached the fence, he discovered that the bars were down. Rufe had forgotten to replace them that afternoon when he drove in the cow to be milked. Despite his absorption, Birt paused to put them up, remembering the vagrant mountain cattle that might stray in upon the corn. He found the familiar little job difficult enough, for it seemed to him that there was never before so black a night. Even looking upward, he could not see the great wind-tossed boughs of the chestnut-oak above his head. He only knew they were near, because acorns dropped upon the rail in his hands, and rebounded resonantly. But an owl, blown helplessly down the gale, was not much better off, for all its vaunted nocturnal vision. As it drifted by, on the currents of the wind, its noiseless, out-

stretched wings, vainly flapping, struck Birt
suddenly in the face, and frightened by the
collision, it gave an odd, peevish squeak.

Birt, too, was startled for a moment. Then
he exclaimed irritably, "Oh, g'way ow*el*" —
realizing what had struck him.

The next moment he paused abruptly. He
thought he heard, close at hand, amongst the
glooms, a faint chuckle. Something — was it?
— *somebody* laughing in the darkness?

He stood intently listening. But now he
heard only the down-pour of the rain, the so-
norous gusts of the wind, the multitudinous
voices of the muttering leaves.

He said to himself that it was fancy. " All
this trouble ez I hev hed along o' Nate Griggs
hev mighty nigh addled my brains."

The name recalled his resolve.

" I 'll git even with him, though. I 'll git
even with him yit," he reiterated as he plodded
on heavily down the path, his mind once more
busy with all the details of his discovery, his
misplaced confidence, and the wreck of his
hopes.

It seemed so hard that he should never before have heard of "entering land," and of that law of the State according priority to the finder of mineral. The mine was his, but he had hid the discovery from all but Nate, who claimed it himself, and had secured the legal title.

"But I'll git even with him," he said resolutely between his set teeth.

He had thought it a lucky chance to remember, in his reverie before the fire-lit hearth, that peg in the shed at the tanyard on which Tim had hung his brother's coat. Somehow the episode of the afternoon had left so vivid an impression on Birt's mind that hours afterward he seemed to see the dull, clouded sky, the sombre, encircling woods, the brown stretch of spent tan, the little gray shed, and within it, hanging upon a peg, the butternut jeans coat, a stiff white paper protruding from its pocket.

That grant, he thought, had taken from him his rights. He would destroy it — he would tear it into bits, and cast it to the turbulent mountain winds. It was not his, to be sure. But was it justly Nate's? — he had no right to enter the land down the ravine.

And so Birt argued with his conscience.

Now wherever Conscience calls a halt, it is no place for Reason to debate the question. The way ahead is no thoroughfare.

Birt did not recognize the tearing of the paper as stealing, but he knew that all this was morally wrong, although he would not admit it. He would not forego his revenge — it was too dear; he was too deeply injured. In the anger that possessed his every faculty, he did not appreciate its futility.

There were other facts which he did *not* know. He was ignorant that the deed which he contemplated was a crime in the estimation of the law, a penitentiary offense.

And toward this terrible pitfall he trudged in the darkness, saying over and again to himself, " I 'll git even with Nate Griggs; he 'll hev no grant, no land, no gold — no more 'n me. I 'll git even with him."

His progress seemed incredibly slow as he

groped along the path. But the rain soon
ceased; the wind began to scatter the clouds;
through a rift he saw a great, glittering planet
blazing high above their dark turmoils.

How the drops pattered down as the wind
tossed the laurel! — once they sounded like
footfalls close behind him. He turned and
looked back into the obscurities of the forest.
Nothing — a frog had begun to croak far
away, and the vibrations of the katydid were
strident on the damp air.

And here was the tanyard, a denser area of
gloom marking where the house and shed
stood in the darkness. He did not hesitate.
He stepped over the bars, which lay as usual
on the ground, and walked across the yard to
the shed. The eaves were dripping with moisture. But the coat, still hanging within on
the peg, was dry.

He had a thrill of repulsion when he
touched it. His hand fell.

" But look how Nate hev treated me," he
remonstrated with his conscience.

The next moment he had drawn the grant

half-way out of the pocket, and as he moved he almost stepped upon something close behind him. All at once he knew what it was, even before a flash of the distant lightning revealed a little tow-head down in the darkness, and a pair of black eyes raised to his in perfect confidence.

It was the little sister who had followed him to-night, as she always did when she could.

"Stand back thar, Tennessee!" he faltered.

He was trembling from head to foot. And yet Tennessee was far too young to tell that she had seen the grant in his hands, to understand, even to question. But had he been seized by the whole Griggs tribe, he could not have been so panic-stricken as he was by the sight of that unknowing little head, the touch of the chubby little hand on his knee.

He thrust the grant back into the pocket of Nate's coat. His resolve was routed by the presence of love and innocence. Not here — not now could he be vindictive, malicious. With some urgent, inborn impulse strongly constraining him, he caught the little sister in his arms, and fled headlong through the darkness, homeward.

As he went he was amazed that he should have contemplated this revenge.

" Why, I can't afford ter be a scoundrel an' sech, jes' 'kase Nate Griggs air a tricky feller an' hev fooled me. Ef Tennessee hed n't stepped up so powerful peart I mought n't hev come ter my senses in time. I mought hev tore up Nate's grant by now. But arter this I ain't never goin' ter set out ter act like a scamp jes' 'kase somebody else does."

His conscience had prevailed, his better self returned. And when he reached home, and opening the door saw his mother still nodding over her knitting, and Rufe asleep in his chair, and the fire smouldering on the hearth, all as he had left it, he might have thought that he had dreamed the temptation and his rescue, but for his dripping garments and Tennessee in his arms all soaking with the rain.

The noise of his entrance roused his mother, who stared in drowsy astonishment at the bedraggled apparition on the threshold.

" Tennie follered me ter the tanyard 'fore I fund her out," Birt explained. " It 'pears ter hev rained on her, considerable," he added deprecatingly.

Tennie was looking eagerly over her shoulder to note the effect of this statement. Her streaming hair flirted drops of water on the floor; her cheeks were ruddy; her black eyes brightened with apprehension.

" Waal, sir! that thar child beats all! Never mind, Tennie, ye 'll meet up with a wild varmint some day when ye air follerin' Birt off from the house, an' I ain't surprised none ef it eats ye! But shucks! " Mrs. Dicey continued impersonally, " I mought ez well save my breath; Tennie ain't feared o' nuthin', ef Birt air by."

The word " varmint " seemed to recall something to Tennessee. She began to chatter unintelligibly about an " ow*el*," and to chuckle so, that Birt had sudden light upon that mysterious laugh which he had heard behind him at the bars.

In his pride in Tennessee he related how

the owl had startled him, and the little girl, invisible in the darkness, had laughed.

" Tennessee ain't pretty, I know, but she air powerful peart," he said, affectionately, as he placed her upon her feet on the floor.

Birt was out early with his axe the next day. The air was delightfully pure after the rain-storm; the sky, gradually becoming visible, wore the ideal azure; the freshened foliage seemed tinted anew. And the morning was pierced by the gilded, glittering javelins of the sunrise, flung from over the misty eastern mountains. As the day dawned all sylvan fascinations were alert in the woods. The fragrant winds were garrulous with wild legends of piney gorges; of tumultuous cascades fringed by thyme and mint and ferns. Every humble weed lent odorous suggestions. The airy things all took to wing. And the spider was a-weaving.

Birt had felled a slender young ash, and was cutting it into lengths for the fireplace, when he noticed a squirrel, sleek woodland dandy, frisking about a rotten log at some little distance, by the roadside.

Suddenly the squirrel paused, then nimbly sped away. There was the sound of approaching hoofs along the road, and presently from around the curve a woman appeared mounted on a sorrel mare, and with a long-legged colt ambling in the rear.

It was Mrs. Griggs, setting out on a journey of some ten miles to visit her married daughter who lived on a neighboring spur. She had taken an early start to "git rid o' the heat o' the noon," as she explained to Mrs. Dicey, who had run out to the rail fence when she reined up beside it. Birt dropped his axe and joined them, expecting to hear more about Nate's grant and the gold mine. Rufe and Tennessee added their company without any definite intention. Pete and Joe were hurrying out of the house toward the group. All the dogs congregated, some of them climbing over the fence to investigate the colt, which was skittish under the ordeal. Even the turkey-gobbler, strutting on the outskirts of the assemblage, had an attentive aspect, as if he, too, relished the gossip.

8

Mrs. Griggs's pink calico sunbonnet sur-
mounted the cap with the explanatory ruffle.
She carried a fan of turkey feathers, and with
appropriate gesticulation, it aided in expound-
ing to Mrs. Dicey the astonishing news that
Nate had found a gold mine on vacant land,
and had entered the tract. They intended to
send specimens to the State Assayer, and they
were all getting ready to begin work at once.

Another surprise to Birt! The ignorant
mountain boy had never heard of the Assayer.
But indeed Nate had only learned of the existence of the office and its uses during that
memorable trip to Sparta.

The prideful Mrs. Griggs from her eleva-
tion, literal and metaphorical, supplemented
all this by the creditable statements that Nate
had turned twenty-one, had cast his vote, and
had a right to a choice at the Cross-roads.

Then she chirruped to the rawboned sorrel
mare, and jogged off down the road, followed
by the frisky colt, whose long, slender legs
when in motion seemed so fragile that it was
startling to witness the temerity with which he

kicked up his frolicsome heels. The dogs, with that odd canine affectation of having just perceived the intruders, pursued them with sudden asperity, barking and snapping, and at last came trotting nimbly home, wagging their tails and with a dutiful mien.

Mrs. Dicey went back into the house, and sat for a time in envious meditation, fairly silenced, and with her apron flung over her face. Then she fell to lamenting that she had been working all her life for nothing, and it would take so little to make the family comfortable, and that her children seemed " disabled somehow in thar heads, an' though always rootin' around in the woods, hed never fund no gold mine nor nuthin' else out o' the common."

Birt kept silent, but the gloom and trouble in his face suddenly touched her heart.

" Thar now, Birt! " she exclaimed, with a world of consolation in her tones, " I don't mean ter say that, nuther. Ain't I a-thinkin' day an' night o' how smart ye be — stiddy an' sensible an' hard-workin' jes' like a man — an' what a good son ye hev been to me ! An'

the t'other chill'n air good too, an' holps me
powerful, though Rufe air hendered some, by
the comical natur o' the critter."

She broke out with a cheerful laugh, in
which Birt could not join.

"An' I mus' be gittin' breakfus fur the
chill'n," she said, kneeling down on the hearth,
and uncovering the embers which had been
kept all night under the ashes.

" Don't ye fret, sonny. I ain't goin' ter
grudge Nate his gold mine. I reckon sech a
good son ez ye be, an' a gold mine too, would
be too much luck fur one woman. Don't ye
fret, sonny."

Birt's self-control gave way abruptly. He
rose in great agitation, and started toward the
door. Then he paused, and broke forth with
passionate incoherence, telling amidst sobs and
tears the story of the woodland's munificence
to him, and how he had flung the gift away.

In recounting the hopes that had deluded
him, the fears that had gnawed, and the despair in which they were at last merged, he
did not notice, for a time, her look as she still

knelt motionless before the embers on the hearth.

He faltered, and grew silent; then stared dumbly at her.

She seemed as one petrified. Her face had blanched; its lines were as sharp and distinct as if graven in stone; only her eyes spoke, an eloquent anguish. Her faculties were numbed for a moment. But presently there was a quiver in her chin, and her voice rang out.

And yet did she understand? did she realize the loss of the mine? For it was not this that she lamented!

"Birt Dicey!" she cried in an appalled tone. "Did ye hide it from yer *mother* — an' tell *Nate Griggs?*"

Birt hung his head. The folly of it!

"What ailed ye, ter hide it from me?" she asked deprecatingly, holding out her worn, hard-working hands. "Hev I ever done ye harm?"

"Nuthin' but good."

"Don't everybody know a boy's mother air bound ter take his part agin all the worl'?"

"Everybody but me," said the penitent Birt.

"What ailed ye, ter hide it from me? What did ye 'low I 'd do?"

"I 'lowed ye would n't want me ter go pardners with Nate," he said drearily.

"I reckon I would n't!" she admitted.

"Ye always said he war a snake in the grass."

"He hev proved that air a true word."

"I wisht I hed n't tole him!" cried Birt vainly. "I wisht I hed n't."

He watched her with moody eyes as she rose at last with a sigh and went mechanically about her preparations for breakfast.

There was a division between them. He felt the gulf widening.

"I jes' wanted it fur you-uns, ennyhow," he said, defending his motives. "I 'lowed ez I mought make enough out'n it ter buy a horse."

"I hain't got time ter sorrow 'bout'n no gold mine," she said loftily. "I used ter believe ye set a heap o' store by yer mother, an'

war willin' ter trust her — ye an' me hevin'
been through mighty hard times together. But
ye don't — I reckon ye never did. I hev los'
mo' than enny gold mine."

And this sorrow for a vanished faith resolved itself into tears with which she salted
her humble bread.

CHAPTER VIII.

IF she had had any relish for triumph, she might have found it in Birt's astonishment to learn that she understood all the details of entering land, which had been such a mystery to him.

" 'T war the commonest thing in the worl', whenst I war young, ter hear 'bout'n folks enterin' land," she said. " But nowadays thar ain't no talk 'bout'n it sca'cely, 'kase the best an' most o' the land in the State hev all been tuk up an' entered — 'ceptin' mebbe a trac', hyar an' thar, full o' rock, an' so steep 't ain't wuth payin' the taxes on."

Simple as she was, she could have given him valuable counsel when it was sorely needed.

He hung about the house later than was his wont, bringing in the store of wood for her work during the day, and "packing" the

water from the spring, with the impulse in his
attention to these little duties to make what
amends he might.

When at last he started for the tanyard, he
knew by the sun that he was long over-due.
He walked briskly along the path through
the sassafras and sumach bushes, on which
the rain-drops still clung. He was presently
brushing them off in showers, for he had
begun to run. It occurred to him that this
was no time to seem even a trifle remiss in his
work at the tanyard. Since he had lost all
his hopes down the ravine, the continuance of
Jube Perkins's favor and the dreary routine
with the mule and the bark-mill were his best
prospects. It would never do to offend the
tanner now.

"With sech a pack o' chill'n ter vittle ez
we-uns hev got at our house," he muttered.

As he came crashing through the underbrush into view of the tanyard, he noticed instantly that it did not wear its usual simple,
industrial aspect. A group of excited men
were standing in front of the shed, one of
them gesticulating wildly.

And running toward the bars came Tim Griggs, panting and white-faced, and exclaiming incoherently at the sight of Birt.

"Oh, Birt," he cried, "I war jes' startin' to yer house arter you-uns; they tole me to go an' fetch ye. Fur massy's sake, gimme Nate's grant. I 'm fairly afeared o' him. He 'll break every bone I own." He held out his hand. "Gimme the grant!"

"Nate's grant!" exclaimed Birt aghast. "I hain't got it! I hain't" —

He paused abruptly. He could not say that he had not touched it.

Tim's wits were sharpened by the keen anxiety of the crisis. He noticed the hesitation. "Ye hev hed it," he cried wildly. "Ye know ye hev been foolin' with it. Ye know 't war you-uns!"

He changed to sudden appeal. "Don't put the blame off on me, Birt," he pleaded. "I 'm fairly afeared o' Nate."

"Ain't the grant in the pocket o' his coat — whar ye left it hangin' on a peg in the shed?" asked Birt, dismayed.

"Naw — naw!" exclaimed Tim, despairingly. "He missed his coat this mornin', bein' the weather war cooler, an' then the grant, an' he sent me arter it. An' I fund the coat a-hangin' thar on the peg, whar I hed lef' it, bein' ez I furgot it when I went off with Rufe ter look at his chickens, an' the pocket war empty an' the paper gone! Nate hev kem ter sarch, too!"

Once more he held out his hand. "Gimme the grant. Nate 'lows 't war you-uns ez tuk it, bein' ez I lef' it hyar."

Birt flushed angrily. "I'll say a word ter Nate Griggs!" he declared.

And he pushed past the trembling Tim, and took his way briskly into the tanyard.

There was a vague murmur in the group as he approached, and Nate Griggs came out from its midst, nodding his head threateningly. His hat, thrust far back on his sandy hair, left in bold relief his long, thin face with its small eyes, which seemed now so close together that his glance had the effect of a squint. He scanned Birt narrowly.

This was the first time the two had met since Birt's ill-starred confidence there by the bark-mill.

" What ails ye, ter 'low ez it air *me* ez hev got yer grant, Nate Griggs?" Birt asked, steadily meeting the accusation.

The excitement had impaired for the moment Nate Griggs's cunning.

"'Kase," he blurted out, "ye hev been a-tryin' ter purtend ez ye fund the mine fust, an' hev been a-tellin' folks 'bout'n it."

"Prove it," said Birt, in sudden elation. " Who war it I tole, an' when?"

The sly Nathan caught his breath with a gasp. His craft had returned.

Admit that to *him* Birt had divulged the discovery of the mine! Confess, when! This would invalidate the entry!

" Ye tole *Tim*," Nate said shamelessly, "an' ez ter when — 't war yestiddy evenin' at the tanyard. Did n't he, Tim?" And he whirled around to his younger brother for confirmation of this audacious and deliberate false-hood.

The abject Tim — poor tool! — frightened
and cowering, nodded to admit it. "Gimme
the grant, Birt," he faltered, helplessly. "I
ought n't ter hev furgot it."

"Look-a-hyar, Birt," said the tanner with
a solemnity which the boy did not altogether
understand, "gin Nate the grant."

"I hain't got it," replied Birt, badgered
and growing nervous.

"Tell him, then, ye never teched it."

Birt's impulse was to adopt the word. But
he had seen enough of falsehood. He had
done with concealment.

"I did tech it," he said boldly, "but I hain't
got it. I put it back in the pocket o' the
coat."

Jube Perkins laid a sudden hand upon his
collar. "'Tain't no use denyin' it, Birt," he
said with the sharp cadence of dismay. "Gin
the grant back ter Nate, an' mebbe he won't
go no furder 'bout'n it. Stealin' a paper like
that air a pen'tiary crime!"

Birt reeled under the word. He thought of
his mother, the children. He had a bitter

foretaste of the suspense, the fear, the humili-
ation. And he was helpless. For no one
would believe him ! His head was in a whirl.
He could not stand. He sank down upon the
wood-pile, vaguely hearing a word here and
there of what was said in the crowd.

" His mother air a widder-woman," remarked one of the group. " An' she air
mighty poor."

Andy Byers was laughing cynically.

Absorbed though he was, Birt experienced
a subacute wonder that any one could feel so
bitterly toward him as to laugh at a moment
like this. How had he made Andy Byers his
enemy !

Nobody noticed it, for Nate was swaggering
about in the crowd, enjoying this conspicuous
opportunity to display all the sophistications
he had acquired in his recent trip to Sparta.
He was calling upon them to witness that he
did not care for the loss of the grant — the
paper was nothing to him ! — for it was on
record in the land office, and he could get a
certified copy from the register in no time at

NATE WAS SWAGGERING ABOUT IN THE CROWD. See page 126.

ill. But his rights were his *rights !* — and ten thousand Diceys should not trample on them. Birt had doubtless thought, being ignorant, that he could destroy the title by making away with the paper; and if there was law in the State, he should suffer for it.

And after this elaborate rodomontade, Nate strode out of the tanyard, with the obsequious Tim following humbly.

Birt told his story again and again, to satisfy curious questioners during the days that ensued. And when he had finished they would look significantly at one another, and chuckle incredulously.

The tanner seemed to earnestly wish to befriend him, and urged him to confess. "The truth 's the only thing ez kin save ye, Birt."

"I 'm tellin' the truth," poor Birt would declare.

Then Jube Perkins argued the question: "How kin ye expec' ennybody ter b'lieve ye when ye say Tennessee purvented ye from takin' the grant — ennything the size o' leetle Tennie, thar."

And he pointed at the little sister, who was perched upon the wood-pile munching an Indian peach.

Somehow Birt did not accurately define the moral force which she had wielded, for he was untaught, and clumsy of speech, and could not translate his feelings. And Jube Perkins was hardly fitted to understand that subtle coercion of affection.

When he found that Birt would only reiterate that Tennie "kem along unbeknown an' purvented " him, Jube Perkins gave up the effort at last, convinced of his guilt.

And Andy Byers said that he was not surprised, for he had known for some little time that Birt was a " most *mischievous* scamp."

Only his mother believed in him, requiting his lack of confidence in her with a fervor of faith in him that, while it consoled, nevertheless cut him to the heart. It has been many years since then, for all this happened along in the fifties, but Birt has never forgotten how staunchly she upheld him in every thought when all the circumstances belied him. Now

that misfortune had touched him, every trace
of her caustic moods had disappeared; she
was all gentleness and tenderness toward him.
And day by day as he went to his work, meeting everywhere a short word, or a slighting
look, he felt that he could not have borne up,
save for the knowledge of that loyal heart at
home.

He was momently in terror of arrest, and
he often pondered on Nate's uncharacteristic
forbearance. Perhaps Nate was afraid that
Birt's story, told from the beginning in court,
might constrain belief and affect the validity
of the entry.

Birt vainly speculated, too, upon the strange
disappearance of the grant. There it was in
the pocket of the coat late that night, and the
next morning early — gone!

Sometimes he suspected that Nate had only
made a pretense of losing the grant, in order
to accuse him and prejudice public opinion
against him, so that he might not be believed
should he claim the discovery of the mineral
down the ravine.

9

His mother sought to keep him from dwelling upon his troubles. "We won't cross the bredge till we git thar," she said. "Mebbe thar ain't none ahead." But her fears for his sake tortured her silent hours when he was away. When he came back from his work, there always awaited him a bright fire, a good supper, and cheerful words as well, although these were the most difficult to prepare. The dogs bounded about him, Tennessee clung to his hand, the boys were hilarious and loud.

By reason of their mother's silence on the subject, that Birt might be better able to go, and work, and hold up his head among the men who suspected him, the children for a time knew nothing of what had happened.

Now Rufe, although his faults were many and conspicuous, was not lacking in natural affection. Had he understood that a cloud overhung Birt, he could not have been so merry, so facetious, so queerly and quaintly bad as he was on his visits to the tanyard, which were peculiarly frequent just now. If Birt had had the heart for it, he might have enjoyed ome of Rufe's pranks at the expense of Andy Byers. The man had once found a sort of entertainment in making fun of Rufe, and this had encouraged the small boy to retaliate as best he could.

At this time, however, Byers suddenly became the gravest of men. He took little notice of the wiles of his elfish antagonist, and whenever he fell into a snare devised by Rufe, he was irritable for a moment, and had forgotten it the next. He had never a word or glance for Birt, who marveled at his conduct. He seemed perpetually brooding upon some perplexity. Occasionally in the midst of his work he would stand motionless for five minutes, the two-handled knife poised in his grasp, his eyes fixed upon the ground, his shaggy brows heavily knitted, his expression doubting, anxious.

The tanner commented upon this inactivity, one day. "Hev ye tuk root thar, Andy?" he asked.

Byers roused himself with a start. "Naw," he replied reflectively, "but I hev been troubled in my mind some, lately, an' I gits ter studyin' powerful wunst in a while."

As he bent to his work, scraping the two-handled knife up and down the hide stretched over the wooden horse, he added, "I hev got so ez I can't relish my vittles sca'cely, bein' so tormented in my mind, an' my sleep air plumb broke up; 'pears like ter me ez I hev got a reg'lar gift fur the nightmare."

"Been skeered by old Mis' Price's harnt lately?" Rufe asked suddenly from his perch upon the wood-pile.

Byers whirled round abruptly, fixing an astonished gaze upon Rufe, unmindful that the knife slipped from his grasp, and fell clanking upon the ground.

CHAPTER IX.

THIS grave, eager gaze Rufe returned with the gayest audacity.

"Been skeered by old Mis' Price's harnt lately?" he once more chirped out gleefully.

He was comical enough, as he sat on the top of the wood-pile, hugging his knees with both arms, his old, bent, wool hat perched on the back of his tow head, and all his jagged squirrel teeth showing themselves, unabashed, in a wide grin.

Jubal Perkins laughed lazily, as he looked at him.

Then, with that indulgence which Rufe always met at the tanyard, and which served to make him so pert and forward, the tanner said, humoring the privileged character, "What be you-uns a-talkin' 'bout, boy? Mrs. Price ain't dead."

"*He* hev viewed old Mis' Price's harnt," cried Rufe, pointing at Andy Byers, with a jocosely crooked finger. "*He* air so peart an' forehanded a-viewin' harnts, he don't hev to wait till folkses be dead. *He* hev seen Mis' Price's harnt — an' it plumb skeered the wits out'n him."

Perkins did not understand this. His interest was suddenly alert. He took his pipe from his mouth, and glanced over his shoulder at Byers. "What air Rufe aimin' at, Andy?" he asked, surprised.

Byers did not reply. He still gazed steadfastly at Rufe ; the knife lay unheeded on the ground at his feet, and the hide was slipping from the wooden horse.

At last he said slowly, "Birt tole ye 'bout'n it, eh?"

"Naw, sir! Naw!" Rufe rocked himself fantastically to and fro in imminent peril of toppling off the wood-pile. "'T war Tom Byers ez tole me."

"*Tom!*" exclaimed Byers, with a galvanic start.

For Tom was his son, and he had not suspected filial treachery in the matter of the
spectral blackberry bush.

Rufe stared in his turn, not comprehending
Byers's surprise.

" *Tom*," he reiterated presently, with mock-
ing explicitness. " Tom Byers — I reckon ye
knows him. That thar freckled-faced, snag-
gled-toothed, red-headed Tom Byers, ez lives
at yer house. I reckon ye *mus'* know him."

" Tom tole ye — *what ?* " asked the tanner,
puzzled by Byers's grave, anxious face, and
Rufe's mysterious sneers.

Rufe broke into the liveliest cackle. " Tom,
he 'lowed ter me ez he war tucked up in the
trundle-bed, fast asleep, that night when his
dad got home from old Mis' Price's house, whar
he had been ter hear her las' words. Tom, he
'lowed he war dreamin' ez his gran'dad hed
gin him a calf — Tom say the calf war spotted
red an' white — an' jes' ez he war a-leadin' it
home with him, his dad kem racin' inter the
house with sech a rumpus ez woke him up, an'
he never got the calf along no furder than the

turn in the road. An' thar sot his dad in the cheer, declarin' fur true ez he hed seen old Mis' Price's harnt in the woods, an' b'lieved she mus' be dead afore now. An' though thar war a right smart fire on the h'a'th, he war shiverin' an' shakin' over it, jes' the same ez ef he war out at the wood-pile, pickin' up chips on a frosty mornin'."

And Rufe crouched over, shivering in every limb, in equally excellent mimicry of a ghost-seer, or an unwilling chip-picker under stress of weather.

"My!" he exclaimed with a fresh burst of laughter; "whenst Tom tole me 'bout'n it I war so tickled I war feared I 'd fall. I los' the use o' my tongue. I could n't stop laffin' long enough ter tell Tom what I war laffin' at. An' ez Tom knowed I war snake-bit las' June, he went home an' tole his mother ez the p'ison hed done teched me in the head, an' said he reckoned, ef the truth war knowed, I hed fits ez a constancy. I say — *fits!*"

Once more the bewildered tanner glanced from one to the other.

"Why, ye never tole me ez ye hed seen su'thin' strange in the woods, Andy," he exclaimed, feeling aggrieved, thus balked of a sensation. "An' the old woman ain't dead, nohow," he continued reasonably, "but air strengthenin' up amazin' fast."

"Waal," put in Rufe, hastening to explain this discrepancy in the spectre, "I hearn youuns a-sayin' that mornin', fore ye set out from the tanyard, ez she war mighty nigh dead an' would be gone 'fore night. An' ez he hed tole me he'd skeer the wits out'n me, I 'lowed ez I could show him ez his wits warn't ez tough ez mine. Though," added the roguish Rufe, with a grin of enjoyment, "arter I hed dressed up the blackberry bush in mam's apron an' shawl, an' sot her bonnet a-top, it tuk ter noddin' and bowin' with the wind, an' looked so like folks, ez it gin *Me* a skeer, an' I jes' run home ez hard ez I could travel. An Towse, he barked at it!"

Andy Byers spoke suddenly. "Waal, Birt holped ye, then."

"He never!" cried Rufe, emphatically, unwilling to share the credit, or perhaps discredit, of the enterprise. "Birt dunno nuthin' 'bout it ter this good day." Rufe winked slyly. "Birt would tell mam ez I hed been a-foolin' with her shawl an' bonnet."

Andy Byers still maintained a most incongruous gravity.

"It warn't Birt's doin', at all?" he said interrogatively, and with a pondering aspect.

Jubal Perkins broke into a derisive guffaw. "What ails ye, Andy?" he cried. "Though ye never seen no harnt, ye 'pear ter be fairly witched by that thar tricked-out blackberry bush."

Rufe shrugged up his shoulders, and began to shiver in imaginary terror over a fancied fire.

" Old — Mis' — Price's — harnt! " he wheezed.

The point of view makes an essential difference. Jube Perkins thought Rufe's comicality most praiseworthy — his pipe went out while he laughed. Byers flushed indignantly.

"Ye aggervatin' leetle varmint!" he cried suddenly, his patience giving way.

He seized the crouching mimic by the collar, and although he did not literally knock him off the wood-pile, as Rufe afterward declared, he assisted the small boy through the air with a celerity that caused Rufe to wink very fast and catch his breath, when he was deposited, with a shake, on the soft pile of ground bark some yards away.

Rufe was altogether unhurt, but a trifle subdued by this sudden aerial excursion. The fun was over for the present. He gathered himself together, and went demurely and sat down on the lowest log of the wood-pile. After a little he produced a papaw from his pocket, and by the manner in which they went to work upon it, his jagged squirrel teeth showed that they were better than they looked.

Towse had followed his master to the tanyard, and was lying asleep beside the woodpile, with his muzzle on his forepaws.

He roused himself suddenly at the sound of munching, and came and sat upright, facing Rufe, and eying the papaw gloatingly. He wagged his tail in a beguiling fashion, and now and then turned his head blandishingly askew.

Of course he would not have relished the papaw, and only begged as a matter of habit or perhaps on principle; but he was given no opportunity to sample it, for Rufe hardly noticed him, being absorbed in dubiously watching Andy Byers, who was once more at work, scraping the hide with the two-handled knife.

Jubal Perkins had gone into the house for a coal to re-kindle his pipe, for there is always a smouldering fire in the "smoke-room" for the purpose of drying the hides suspended from the rafters. He came out with it freshly glowing, and sat down on the broad, high pile of wood.

As the first whiff of smoke wreathed over his head, he said, "What air the differ ter ye, Andy, whether 't war bub, hyar, or Birt, ez dressed up the blackberry bush? ye 'pear ter make a differ a-twixt 'em."

Still Byers was evasive. "Whar's Birt, ennyhow?" he demanded irrelevantly.

"Waal," drawled the tanner, with a certain

constraint, " I hed been promisin' Birt a day
off fur a right smart while, an' I tole him ez
he mought ez well hev the rest o' ter-day. He
'lowed ez he warn't partic'lar 'bout a day off,
now. But I tole him ennyhow ter go along.
I seen him a while ago passin' through the
woods, with his rifle on his shoulder — gone
huntin', I reckon."

" *Gone huntin' !* " ejaculated Rufe in dud-
geon, joining unceremoniously in the conversation of his elders. " Now, Birt mought hev
let me know! I 'd hev wanted ter go along
too."

" Mebbe that air the reason he never tole
ye, bub," said Perkins dryly.

For he could appreciate that Rufe's society
was not always a boon, although he took a
lenient view of the little boy. Any indulgence of Birt was more unusual, and Andy
Byers experienced some surprise to hear of
the unwonted sylvan recreations of the young
drudge. He noticed that the mule was off
duty too, grazing among the bushes just beyond the fence, and hobbled so that he could

not run away. This precaution might have seemed a practical joke on the mule, for the poor old animal was only too glad to stand stock still.

Rufe continued his exclamatory indignation.

"Jes' ter go lopin' off inter the woods huntin', 'thout lettin' *Me* know! An' I never gits ter go huntin' nohow! An' mam won't let me tech Birt's rifle, 'thout it air ez empty ez a gourd! She say she air feared I'll shoot my head off, an' she don't want no boys, 'thout heads, jouncin' round her house — shucks! Which way did Birt take, Mister Perkins? — 'kase I be goin' ter ketch up."

"He war headed fur that thar salt lick, whenst I las' seen him," replied the tanner; " ef ye stir yer stumps right lively, mebbe ye'll overhaul him yit."

Rufe rose precipitately. Towse, believing his petition for the papaw was about to be rewarded, leaped up too, gamboling with a display of ecstasy that might have befitted a starving creature, and an elasticity to be expected only of a rubber dog. As he uttered a shrill yelp of delight, he sprang up against Rufe, who, reeling under the shock, dropped the remnant of the papaw. Towse darted upon it, sniffed disdainfully, and returned to his capers around Rufe, evidently declining to believe that all that show of gustatory satisfaction had been elicited only by the papaw, and that Rufe had nothing else to eat.

Thus the two took their way out of the tanyard ; and even after they had disappeared, their progress through the underbrush was marked by an abnormal commotion among the leaves, as the saltatory skeptic of a dog insisted on more substantial favors than the succulent papaw.

The tanner smoked for a time in silence.

Then, " Birt ain't goin' ter be let ter work hyar ag'in," he said.

Byers elevated his shaggy eyebrows in surprise.

" Ye see," said the tanner in a confidential undertone, " sence Birt hev stole that thar grant, I kin argufy ez he mought steal su'thin'

else, an' I ain't ekal ter keepin' up a spry lookout on things, an' bein' partic'lar 'bout the
count o' the hides an' sech. I can't feel easy
with sech a mischeevious scamp around."

Byers made no rejoinder, and the tanner,
puffing his pipe, vaguely watched the wreaths
of smoke rise above his head, and whisk buoy-
antly about in the air, and finally skurry off
into invisibility. A gentle breeze was astir in
the woods, and it set the leaves to whispering.
The treetoads and the locusts were trolling a
chorus. So loudly vibrant, it was! So clam-
orously gay! Some subtle intimation they
surely had that summer was ephemeral and
the season waning, for the burden of their
song was, Let us now be merry. The scarlet
head of a woodpecker showed brilliantly from
the bare dead boughs of a chestnut-oak, which,
with its clinging lichens of green and gray,
was boldly projected against the azure sky.
And there, the filmy moon, most dimly visible
in the afternoon sunshine, swung like some
lunar hallucination among the cirrus clouds.

"Ye 'lows ez I ain't doin' right by Birt?"

the tanner suggested presently, with more conscience in the matter than one would have given him credit for possessing.

"I knows ye air doin' right," said Byers unexpectedly.

All at once the woodpecker was solemnly tapping — tapping.

Byers glanced up, as if to discern whence the sudden sound came, and once more bent to his work.

" Ye b'lieves, then, ez he stole that thar grant from Nate Griggs ? " asked Perkins.

"I be *sure* he done it," said Byers, unequivocally.

The tanner took his pipe from his lips. " What ails ye ter say that, Andy ? " he exclaimed excitedly.

Andy Byers hesitated. He mechanically passed his fingers once or twice across the blunt, curved blade of the two-handled knife.

" Ye 'll keep the secret ? "

" In the sole o' my boot," said the tanner.

" Waal, I *knows* ez Birt stole the grant. I hev been powerful changeful, though, in my

10

thoughts bout'n it. At fust I war glad when he war suspicioned 'bout'n it, an' I war minded to go an' inform on him an' sech, ter pay him back; 'kase I held a grudge ag'in him, believin' ez he hed dressed out that thar blackberry bush ez Mrs. Price's harnt. An' then I'd remember ez his mother war a widderwoman, an' he war nothin' but a boy, an' boys air bound ter be gamesome an' full o' jokes wunst in a while, an' I'd feel like I war bound ter furgive him 'bout the harnt. An' then ag'in I got toler'ble oneasy fur fear the Law mought hold *me* 'sponsible fur knowin' 'bout Birt's crime of stealin' the grant an' yit not tellin' on him. An' I'd take ter hopin' an' prayin' the boy would confess, so ez I wouldn't hev ter tell on him. I hev been mightily pestered in my mind lately with sech dilly-dallyin'."

Again the sudden tapping of the woodpecker filled the pause.

"Did ye *see* him steal the grant, Andy?" asked the tanner, with bated breath.

"Ez good ez seen him. I seen him slyin'

round, an' I *hev fund the place whar he hev hid it.*"

And the woodpecker still was solemnly tapping, high up in the chestnut-oak tree.

CHAPTER X.

BIRT, meanwhile, was trudging along in the woods, hardly seeing where he went, hardly caring.

He had not had even a vague premonition when the tanner told him that he might have the rest of the day off. He did not now want the holiday which would once have so rejoiced him, and he said as much. And then the tanner, making the disclosure by degrees, being truly sorry to part with the boy, intimated that he need come back no more.

Birt unharnessed the mule by the sense of touch and the force of habit, for blinding tears intervened between his vision and the rusty old buckles and worn straps of leather. The animal seemed to understand that something was amiss, and now and then turned his head interrogatively. Somehow Birt was glad to

feel that he left at least one friend in the tanyard, albeit the humblest, for he had always
treated the beast with kindness, and he was
sure the mule would miss him.

When he reached home he loitered for a
time outside the fence, trying to nerve himself
to witness his mother's distress. And at last
his tears were dried, and he went in and told
her the news.

It was hard for him nowadays to understand
that simple mother of his. She did nothing
that he expected. To be sure her cheek paled,
her eyes looked anxious for a moment, and
her hands trembled so that she carefully put
down upon the table a dish which she had
been wiping. But she said quite calmly,
"Waal, sonny, I dunno but ye hed better take
a day off from work, sure enough, an' go
a-huntin'. Thar's yer rifle, an' mebbe ye'll
git a shot at a deer down yander by the lick.
The chill'n haint hed no wild meat lately,
'ceptin' squir'ls out'n Rufe's trap."

And then he began to cry out bitterly that
nobody would give him work, and they would

all starve; that the tanner believed he had stolen the grant, and was afraid to have him about the hides.

" 'T ain't no differ ez long ez 't ain't the truth," said his mother philosophically. " We-uns will jes' abide by the truth."

He repeated this phrase over and over as he struggled through the tangled underbrush of the dense forest.

It was all like some terrible dream; and but for Tennessee, it would be the truth! How he blessed the little sister that her love for him and his love for her had come between him and crime at that moment of temptation.

"So powerful peart!" he muttered with glistening eyes, as he thought of her.

The grant was gone, to be sure; but he did not take it. They accused him — and falsely!

It was something to be free and abroad in the woods. He heard the wind singing in the pines. Their fine, penetrating aroma pervaded the air, and the rusty needles, covering the ground, muffled his tread. Once he paused — was that the bleat of a fawn, away down on the mountain's slope? He heard no more, and he walked on, looking about with his old alert interest. He was refreshed, invigorated, somehow consoled, as he went. O wise mother! he wondered if she foresaw this when she sent him into the woods.

He had not before noted how the season was advancing. Here and there, in the midst of the dark green foliage, leaves shone so vividly yellow that it seemed as if upon them some fascinated sunbeam had expended all its glamours. In a dusky recess he saw the crimson sumach flaring. And the distant blue mountains, and the furthest reaches of the azure sky, and the sombre depths of the wooded valley, and the sheeny splendors of the afternoon sun, and every incident of crag or chasm — all appeared through a soft purple haze that possessed the air, and added an ideal embellishment to the scene. Down the ravine the "lick" shone with the lustre of a silver lakelet. He saw the old oak-tree hard by, with the historic scaffold among its thinning leaves, and further along the slope were visi-

ble vague bobbing figures, which he recognized
as the "Griggs gang," seeking upon the mountain side the gold which he had discovered.

Suddenly he heard a light crackling in the
brush, — a faint footfall.   It reminded him
of the deer-path close at hand.   He crouched
down noiselessly amongst the low growth and
lifted his rifle, his eyes fixed on the point
where the path disappeared in the bushes, and
where he would first catch a glimpse of the
approaching animal.

He heard the step again.   His finger was
trembling on the trigger, when down the path
leisurely walked an old gentleman attired in
black, a hammer in his hand, and a pair of
gleaming spectacles poised placidly upon the
bridge of an intellectual Roman nose.   And
this queer game halted in the middle of the
deer-path, all unconscious of his deadly danger.

It was a wonder that the rifle was not discharged, for the panic-stricken Birt had lost
control of his muscles, and his convulsive finger was still quivering on the trigger as he
trembled from head to foot.   He hardly dared

to try to move the gun. For a moment he could not speak. He gazed in open-mouthed amazement at the unsuspecting old gentleman, who was also unaware of the far more formidable open mouth of the rifle.

"Now, ain't ye lackin' fur head-stuffin'?" suddenly yelled out Birt, from his hiding-place.

The startled old man jumped, with the most abrupt alacrity. In fact, despite his age and the lack of habit, he bounded as acrobatically from the ground as the expected deer could have done. He was, it is true, a learned man; but science has no specific for sudden fright, and he jumped as ignorantly as if he did not know the difficult name of any of the muscles that so alertly exercised themselves on this occasion.

Birt rose at last to his feet and looked with a pallid face over the underbrush. "Now, ain't ye lackin' fur head-stuffin'," he faltered, "a-steppin' along a deer-path ez nat'ral ez ef ye war a big fat buck? I kem mighty nigh shootin' ye."

The old gentleman recovered his equilibrium, mental and physical, with marvelous
rapidity.

"Ah, my young friend," — he motioned to
Birt to come nearer, — "I want to speak to
you."

Birt stared. One might have inferred, from
the tone, that the gentleman had expected to
meet him here, whereas Birt had just had the
best evidence of his senses that the encounter
was a great surprise.

The boy observed his interlocutor more carefully than he had yet been able to do. He
remembered all at once Rufe's queer story of
meeting, down the ravine, an eccentric old
man whom he was disposed to identify as
Satan. As the stranger stood there in the
deer-path, he looked precisely as Rufe had de-
scribed him, even to the baffling glitter of his
spectacles, his gray whiskers, and the curiously
shaped hammer in his hand.

Birt, although bewildered and still tremulous from the shock to his nerves, was not so
superstitious as Rufe, and he shouldered his

gun, and, pushing out from the tangled underbrush, joined the old man in the path.

"I want," said the gentleman, "to hire a
boy for a few days — weeks, perhaps."

He smiled with two whole rows of teeth
that never grew where they stood. Birt wished
he could see the expression of the stranger's
eyes, indistinguishable behind the spectacles
that glimmered in the light.

"What do you say to fifty cents a day?"
he continued briskly.

Birt's heart sank suddenly. He had heard
that Satan traded in souls by working on the
avarice of the victim. The price suggested
seemed a great deal to Birt, for in this region
there is little cash in circulation, barter serving all the ordinary purposes of commerce.

As he hesitated, the old man eyed him quiz-
zically. "Afraid of work, eh?"

"Naw, sir!" said Birt, sturdily.

Ah, if the bark-mill, and the old mule, and
the tan-pit, and the wood-pile, and the cornfield might testify!

"Fifty cents a day — eh?" said the stranger.

At the repetition of the sum, it occurred to Birt, growing more familiar with the eccentricity of his companion, that he ought not in sheer silliness to throw away a chance for employment.

"Kin I ask my mother?" he said dubiously.

"By all means ask your mother," replied the stranger heartily.

Birt's last fantastic doubt vanished. Oh no! this was not Satan in disguise. When did the enemy ever counsel a boy to ask his mother!

Birt still stared gravely at him. All the details of his garb, manner, speech, even the hammer in his hand, were foreign to the boy's experience.

Presently he ventured a question. "Do you-uns hail from hyar-abouts?"

The stranger was frank and communicative. He told Birt that he was a professor of Natural Science in a college in one of the "valley towns," and that he was sojourning, for his health's sake, at a little watering-place some twelve miles distant on the bench of the moun-

tain. Occasionally he made an excursion into
the range, which was peculiarly interesting
geologically.

"But what I wish you to do is to dig for —
bones."

" *Bones ?* " faltered Birt.

"Bones," reiterated the professor solemnly.
Did his spectacles twinkle ?

Birt stood silent, vaguely wondering what
his mother would think of " bones."

Presently the professor, seeing that the boy
was not likely to ask amusing questions, explained.

He informed Birt that in the neighborhood
of salt licks — " saline quagmires " he called
them — were often found the remains of animals of an extinct species, which are of great
value to science. He gave Birt the extremely
long name of these animals, and descanted
upon such conditions of their existence as is
known, much of which Birt did not understand.
Although this fact was very apparent, it did
not in the least affect the professor's ardor in
the theme. He was in the habit of talking of

these things to boys who did not understand, and alack! to boys who did not want to understand.

One point, however, he made very clear. With the hope of some such "find," he was anxious to investigate this particular lick, — about which indeed he had heard a vague tradition of a "big bone" discovery, such as is common to similar localities in this region, — and for this purpose he proposed to furnish the science and the fifty cents *per diem*, and earnestly desired that some one else should furnish the muscle.

He was accustomed to think much more rapidly than the men with whom Birt was associated, and his briskness in arranging the matter had an incongruous suggestion of the giddiness of youth. He said that he would go home with Birt to fetch the spade, and while there he could settle the terms with the boy's mother, and then they could get to work.

He started off at a dapper gait up the deer-path, while Birt, with his rifle on his shoulder, followed.

A sudden thought struck Birt. He stopped short.

"Now *I* dunno which side o' that thar lick Nate Griggs's line runs on," he remarked.

"Never mind," said the professor, waving away objections with airy efficiency; "I shall first secure the consent of the owner of the land."

Birt cogitated for a moment. "Nate Griggs ain't goin' ter gin his cornsent ter nobody ter dig ennywhar down the ravine, ef it air inside o' his lines," he said confidently, "'kase I — 'kase he — leastwise, 'kase gold hev been fund hyar lately, an' he hev entered the land."

The professor stopped short in the path.

"Gold!" he ejaculated. "Gold!"

Was there a vibration of incredulity in his voice?

Birt remembered all at once the specimens which he had picked up that memorable evening, down the ravine, when he shot the red fox. Here they still were in his pocket. They showed lustrous, metallic, yellow gleams as he placed them carefully in the old man's outstretched hand, telling how he came by them, of his mistaken confidence, the betrayed trust, and ending by pointing at the group of gold-seekers, microscopic in the distance on the opposite slope.

"I hev hearn tell," he added, " ez Nate air countin' on goin' pardners with a man in Sparty, who hev got money, to work the gold mine."

Now and then, as he talked, he glanced up at his companion's face, vaguely expecting to discover his opinion by its expression, but the light still played in a baffling glitter upon his spectacles.

Birt could only follow when the professor suddenly handed back the specimens with a peremptory "Come — come! We must go for the spade. But when we reach your mother's house I will test this mineral, and you shall see for yourself what you have lost."

Mrs. Dicey's first impression upon meeting the stranger and learning of his mission was not altogether surprise as Birt had expected. Her chief absorption was a deep thankfulness that the floors all preserved their freshly scoured appearance.

" Fur ef Rufe hed been playin' round hyar ter-day, same ez common, the rubbish would have been a scandal ter the kentry," she reflected.

In fact, all was so neat, albeit so poor, that the stranger felt as polite as he looked, while he talked to her about employing Birt in his researches.

Birt, however, had little disposition to listen to this. He was excited by the prospect of testing the mineral, and he busied himself with great alacrity in preparing for it under the professor's directions. He suffered a qualm, it is true, as he pounded the shining fragments into a coarse powder, and then he drew out with the shovel a great glowing mass of live coals on the hearth.

The dogs peered eagerly in at the door, having followed the stranger with the liveliest curiosity. Towse, bolder than the rest, entered intrepidly with a nonchalant air and a wagging tail, for he and Rufe, having failed to

11

find Birt, had just returned home. The small boy paused on the threshold in amazed recognition of the old gentleman who had occasioned him such a fright that day down the ravine.

The professor gesticulated a great deal as he bent over the fire and gave Birt directions, and, with his waving hands and the glow on his hoary hair and beard, he looked like some fantastic sorcerer. Somehow Rufe was glad to see the familiar countenances of Pete and Joe, and was still more reassured to note that his mother was quietly standing beside the table, as she stirred the batter for bread in a wooden bowl. Tennessee had pressed close to Birt, her chubby hand clutching his collar as he knelt on the hearth. He held above the glowing coals a long fire shovel, on which the pulverized mineral had been placed, and his eyes were very bright as he earnestly watched it.

"If it is gold," said the old man, "a moderate heat will not affect it."

The shovel was growing hot. The live coals glowed beneath it. The breath of the fire

TESTING THE MINERAL.   See page 162.

stirred Tennessee's flaxen hair. And Birt's dilated eyes saw the yellow particles still glistening unchanged in the centre of the shovel, which was beginning to redden.

CHAPTER XI.

SUDDENLY — was the glistening yellow mineral taking fire? It began to give off sulphurous fumes. And drifting away with them were all Birt's golden visions and Nate's ill-gotten wealth — ending in smoke!

The sulphurous odor grew stronger. Even Towse stopped short, and gazed at the shovel with a reprehensive sniff.

"Ker-shoo!" he sneezed.

And commenting thus, he turned abruptly and went hastily out, with a startled look and a downcast tail.

His sneeze seemed to break the spell of silence that had fallen on the little group.

"It be mighty nigh bodaciously changed ter cinders!" exclaimed Birt, staring in amaze at the lustreless contents of the shovel from which every suggestion of golden glimmer had faded. "What do it be, ef 'tain't gold?"

"Iron pyrites," said the professor. "'Fools' gold,' it is often called."

He explained to Birt that in certain formations, however, gold is associated with iron pyrites, and when the mineral is properly roasted, this process serving to expel the sulphur, the fine particles of gold are found held in the resulting oxide of iron. But the variety of the mineral discovered down the ravine he said was valueless, unless occurring in vast quantities, when it is sometimes utilized in the production of sulphur.

"I wonder," Birt broke out suddenly, "if the assayer won't find no gold in them samples ez Nate sent him."

The professor laughed. "The assayer will need the 'philosopher's stone' to find gold in any samples from this locality."

"Ye knowed then, all the time, ez this stuff warn't gold?" asked Birt.

"All the time," rejoined the elder.

"An' Nate hev got the steepest, rockiest spot in the kentry ter pay taxes on," resumed Birt, reflectively. "An' he hev shelled out

a power o' money ter the surveyor, an' sech,
a'ready. I reckon he 'll be mightily outed
when he finds out ez the min'ral ain't gold."

Birt stopped short in renewed anxiety.

That missing grant! Somehow he felt sure
that Nate, balked of the great gains he had
promised himself, would wreak his disappointment wherever he might; and since the land
was of so little value, he would not continue to
deny himself his revenge for fear that an in-
vestigation into the priority of the mineral's
discovery might invalidate the entry. Once
more Birt was tortured by the terror of arrest
— he might yet suffer a prosecution from
malignity, which had hitherto been withheld
from policy. If only the mystery of the lost
grant could be solved!

The conversation of the elders had returned
to the subject of the investigations around the
"lick" and the terms for Birt's services. As
so much time had been consumed with the pyrites, the professor concluded with some vexa-
tion that they could hardly arrange all the
preliminaries and get to work this afternoon.

"I dare say we had best begin to-morrow morning," he said at last.

"Birt can't go a-diggin' no-ways, this evenin'," put in the officious Rufe, who stood, according to his wont, listening with his mouth and eyes wide open, "'kase ez I kem home by the tanyard Jube Perkins hollered ter me ter tell Birt ter come thar right quick. I furgot it till this minit," he added, with a shade of embarrassment that might pass for apology.

Birt felt a prophetic thrill. This summons promised developments of importance. Only a few hours ago he was discharged under suspicion of dishonesty; why this sudden recall? He did not know whether hope or fear was paramount. He trembled with eager expectancy. He seized his hat, and strode out of the house without waiting to hear more of the professor's plans or the details of the wages.

He had reached the fence before he discovered Tennessee close at his heels. He cast his troubled eyes down upon her, and met her pleading, upturned gaze. He was about to charge her to go back. But then he remembered how she had followed him with blessings — how mercy had kept pace with her steps. He would not deny her the simple boon she craved, and if she were troublesome and in his way, surely he might be patient with her, since she loved him so! He lifted her over the fence, and then started briskly down the path, the sturdy, light-footed little mountain girl delightedly trudging along in the rear.

When he entered the tanyard no one was there except Jube Perkins and Andy Byers: the tanner, lounging as usual on the wood-pile, and the workman, with scarcely less the aspect of idleness, dawdlingly scraping a hide on the wooden horse. Birt discerned a portent in the unwonted solemnity of their faces, and his heart sank.

" Waal, Birt, we-uns hev been a-waitin' fur ye," said the tanner in a subdued, grave tone that somehow reminded Birt of the bated voices in a house of death. " Set down hyar on the wood-pile, fur Andy an' me hev got a word ter say ter ye."

Birt's dilated black eyes turned in dumb appeal from one to the other as he sank down on the wood-pile. His suspense gnawed him like an actual grief while Jubal Perkins slowly shifted his position and looked vaguely at Andy Byers for a suggestion, being uncertain how to begin.

"Waal, Birt," he drawled at last, "ez yer dad is dead an' ye hev got nobody ter see arter ye an' advise ye, Andy an' me, we-uns agreed ez how we 'd talk ter ye right plain, an' try ter git ye ter jedge o' this hyar matter like we-uns do. Andy an' me know more 'bout the law, an' 'bout folks too, than ye does. These hyar Griggs folks hev always been misdoubted ez a fractious an' contrary-wise fambly. Ef enny Griggs ain't aggervatin' an captious, it air through bein' plumb terrified by the t'others. They air powerful hard folks — an' they 'll land ye in the State Prison yet, I 'm thinkin'. I wonder they hain't started at ye a'ready. But thar's no countin' on 'em, 'ceptin' that they 'll do all they kin that air ha'sh an' grindin'."

"That air a true word, Birt," said Andy Byers, speaking to the boy for the first time in many days. "Ef they hev thar reason fur it, they mought hold thar hand fur a time, but fust or las' they'll hev all out'n ye ez the law will allow 'em."

Birt listened in desperation. All this was sharpened by the certainty that the mineral was only valueless pyrites, and the prescience of Nate's anger when this fact should come to his knowledge, and prudence no longer restrain him. His rage would vent itself on his luckless victim for every cent, every mill, that the discovery of the "fools' gold" had cost him.

"They'll be takin' ye away from the mountings ter jail ye an' try ye, an' mebbe ye'll go ter the pen'tiary arter that. An' how will yer mother, an' brothers, an' sister, git thar vittles, an' firewood, an' corn-crap an' clothes, an' sech — Rufe bein' the oldest child, arter you-uns?" demanded the tanner. "An' even when ye git back — I hate ter tell ye this word — nobody will want ye round. They'll be feared ye'd be forever pickin' an' stealin'."

" But we-uns will stand up fur ye, bein' ez ye air the widder's son," said Byers eagerly. " We-uns will gin the Griggs tribe ter onderstand that."

" An' mebbe the Griggses won't want ter do nuthin', ef they hain't got no furder cause fur holdin' a grudge," put in the tanner.

" What be ye a-layin' off fur me ter do?" asked Birt wonderingly.

" Ter gin Nate's grant back ter him," they both replied in a breath.

" I hev not got it!" cried poor Birt tumultuously. " I never stole it! I dunno whar it be!"

The tanner's expression changed from paternal kindliness to contemptuous anger.

" Air ye goin' ter keep on bein' a liar, Birt, ez well ez a thief?" he said sternly.

"I dunno whar it be," reiterated Birt desperately.

" *I* know whar it be," said Byers.

Birt gazed at him astounded.

" Whar?" he cried eagerly.

" Whar ye hid it," returned Byers coolly.

Birt's lips moved with difficulty as he husk-
ily ejaculated " I never hid it — I never ! "

" Ye need n't deny it.   I ez good ez seen ye
hide it."

Birt looked dazed for a moment.   Then
the blood rushed to his face and as suddenly
receded, leaving it pale and rigid.   He was
cold and trembling.   He could not speak.

The tanner scrutinized him narrowly.   Then
he said, " Tell him 'bout it, Andy.   Tell him
jes' ez ye tole me.   An' mebbe he 'll hev sense
enough ter gin it up when he sees he air fairly
caught."

" Waal," said Byers, leaning back against
the wall of the smoke-house, and holding the
knife idly poised in his hand, " I kem down
ter the tanyard betimes that mornin' arter the
storm.   Both ye an' Birt war late.   I noticed
Nate Griggs's coat haugin' thar in the shed,
with a paper stickin' out'n the pocket, ez I
started inter the smoke-house ter tend ter the
fire.   I reckon I mus' hev made consider'ble
racket in thar, 'kase I never hearn nuthin' till
I sot down afore the fire on a log o' wood, an'

lit my pipe. All of a suddenty thar kem a
step outside, toler'ble light on the tan. I jes'
'lowed 't war ye or Birt. But I happened ter
look up, an' thar I see a couple o' big black
eyes peepin' through that thar crack in the
wall."

He turned and pointed out a crevice where
the " daubin' " had fallen from the " chinkin' "
between the logs.

" Ye can see," he resumed, " ez this hyar
crack air jes' the height o' Birt. Waal, them
eyes lookin' in so onexpected did n't 'sturb me
none. I hev knowed the Dicey eye fur thirty
year, an' thar ain't none like 'em nowhar round
the mountings. But I 'lowed 't war toler'ble
sassy in Birt ter stand thar peerin' at me
through the chinkin'. I never let on, though,
ez I viewed him. An' then, them eyes jes' set
up sech a outdacious winkin' an' wallin', an'
squinchin', ez I knowed he war makin' faces
at me. So I jes' riz up — an' the eyes slipped
away from thar in a hurry. I war aimin' ter
larrup Birt fur his sass, but I stopped ter
hang up a skin ez I hed knocked down. It

never tuk me long, much, but when I went out, thar war n't nobody ter be seen in the tan-yard."

He paused to place one foot upon the wooden horse, and he leaned forward with a reflective expression, his elbow on his knee, and his hand holding his bearded chin.

The afternoon was waning. The scarlet sun in magnified splendor was ablaze low down in the saffron west. The world seemed languorously afloat in the deep, serene flood of light. Shadows were lengthening slowly. The clangor of a cow-bell vibrated in the distance.

The drone of Andy Byers's voice overbore it as he recommenced.

" Waal, I was sorter conflusticated, an' I looked round powerful sharp ter see whar Birt hed disappeared to. I happened ter cut my eye round at that thar pit ez he hed finished layin' the tan in, an' kivered with boards, an' weighted with rocks that day ez ye an' me hed ter go an' attend on old Mrs. Price. Ye know we counted ez that thar pit would n't be opened ag'in fur a right smart time ? "

The tanner nodded assent.

" Waal, I noticed ez the aidge o' one o' them boards war sot sorter catawampus, an' I 'lowed ez 't war the wind ez hed 'sturbed it. Ez I stooped down ter move it back in its place, I seen su'thin' white under it. So I lifted the board, an' thar I see, lyin' on the tan a-top o' the pit, a stiff white paper. I looked round toward the shed, an' thar hung the coat yit — with *nuthin'* in the pocket. I did n't know edzactly what ter make of it, an' I jes' shunted the plank back over the paper in the pit like I fund it, an' waited ter see what mought happen. An' all the time ez that thar racket war goin' on bout'n the grant, *I* knowed powerful well whar 't war, an' who stole it."

Birt looked from one to the other of the two men. Both evidently believed every syllable of this story. It was so natural, so credible, that he had a curious sense of inclining toward it, too. Had he indeed, in some aberration, taken the grant? Was it some tricksy spirit in his likeness that had peered through the chinking at Andy Byers?

He could find no words to contend further. He sat silent, numb, dumfounded.

" Birt," said the tanner coaxingly, " thar ain't no use in denyin' it enny mo'. Let 's go an' git that grant, an' take it ter Nate an' tell the truth."

The words roused Birt. He clutched at the idea of getting possession of the paper that had so mysteriously disappeared and baffled and eluded him. He could at least return it. And even if this should fail to secure him lenient treatment, he would feel that he had done right. He rose suddenly in feverish anxiety.

Andy Byers and Perkins, exchanging a wink of congratulation, followed him to the pit.

" It air under this hyar board," said Byers, moving one of the heavy stones, and lifting a broad plank.

Perkins pressed forward with eager curiosity, never having seen this famous grant.

The ground bark on the surface was pretty dry, the layer being ten or fifteen inches thick, and the tanning infusion had not yet risen through it.

Byers stared with a frown at the tan, and lifted another board. Nothing appeared beneath it on the smooth surface of the bark.

In sudden alarm they took away the boards, one after another, till all were removed, and the whole surface of the pit was exposed.

Then they looked at each other, bewildered. For once more the grant was gone.

12

CHAPTER XII.

JUBAL PERKINS broke the silence.

"Andy Byers," he exclaimed wrathfully, "what sort 'n tale is this ez ye air tryin' ter fool me with?"

Byers, perturbed and indignant, was instantly ready to accuse Birt.

"Ye hev been hyar an' got the grant an' sneaked it off agin, hev ye!" he cried, scowling at the boy.

Then he turned to the tanner. "I hope I may drap dead, Jube," he said earnestly, "ef that grant war n't right hyar" — he pointed at the spot — "las' night whenst I lef' the tanyard. I always looked late every evenin' ter be sure it hed n't been teched, thinkin' I'd make up my mind in the night whether I'd tell on Birt, or no. But I never could git plumb sati'fied what to do."

ffis tone carried conviction. The tanner looked at Birt with disappointment in every line of his face. There was severity, too, in his expression. He was beginning to admit the fitness of harsh punishment in this case.

"Ye don't wuth all this gabblin' an' jawin' over ye, ye miser'ble leetle critter," he said. "An' I ain't goin' ter waste another breath on ye."

Birt stood vacantly staring at the tan. All the energy of the truth was nullified by the futility of protestation.

The two men exchanged a glance of vague comment upon his silence, and then they too looked idly down at the pit.

Tennessee abruptly caught Birt's listless hand as it hung at his side, for Towse had suddenly entered the tanyard, and prancing up to her in joyous recognition, was trying to lick her face.

"G'way, Towse," she drawled gutturally. She struck vaguely at him with her chubby little fist, which he waggishly took between his teeth in a gingerly gentle grip.

"Stand back thar, Tennessee," Birt murmured mechanically.

As usual, Towse was the precursor of Rufe, who presently dawdled out from the underbrush. He quickened his steps upon observing the intent attitude of the party, and as he came up he demanded vivaciously, "What ails that thar pit o' yourn, Mister Perkins? — thought ye said 't warn't goin' ter be opened ag'in fore-shortly."

For a moment the tanner made no reply. Then he drawled absently, "Nuthin' ails the pit, Rufe — nuthin'."

Rufe sat down on the edge of it, and gazed speculatively at it. Presently he began anew, unabashed by the silence of the grave and contemplative group.

"This hyar tan hev got sorter moist a-top now ; I wonder ef that thar grant o' Nate's got spi'led ennywise with the damp."

Birt winced. It had been a certain mitigation of his trouble that, thanks to his mother's caution, the children at home knew nothing of the disgrace that had fallen upon him, and

RUFF PUTS IN SOME UNEXPECTED EVIDENCE.   See page 180.

that there, at least, the atmosphere was un-
tainted with suspicion.

The next moment he was impressed by the
singularity of Rufe's mention of the missing
grant and its place of concealment.

"Look-a-hyar, Rufe," he exclaimed, excitedly; "how d' ye know ennything 'bout
Nate's grant an' whar 't war hid?"

Rufe glanced up scornfully, insulted in some
occult manner by the question.

"How did I know, Birt Dicey? How d' ye
know yerse'f?" he retorted. "I knows a
heap, ginerally."

Perkins, catching the drift of Birt's intention, came to the rescue.

"Say, bub, how d' ye know the grant war
ever put hyar?"

"Kase," responded Rufe, more amicably,
"I seen it put hyar — right yander."

He indicated the spot where the paper lay,
according to Byers, when it was discovered.

Birt could hardly breathe. His anxieties,
his hopes, his fears, seemed a pursuing pack
before which he was almost spent. ·He panted

like a hunted creature. Tennessee was swinging herself to and fro, holding by his hand. Sometimes she caught at Towse's unlovely ear, as he sat close by with his tongue lolled out and an attentive air, as if he were assisting at the discussion.

" Who put it thar, bub?" demanded Perkins.

It would not have surprised Birt, so perverse had been the course of events, if Rufe had accused him on the spot.

" Pig-wigs Griggs," replied Rufe, unexpectedly.

A glance of intelligence passed between the men.

" Tell 'bout it, Rufe," said the tanner, suppressing all appearance of excitement.

"Ye ain't goin' ter do nuthin' ter Pig-wigs fur foolin' with yer pit, ef I tell ye?" asked Rufe, quickly.

" Naw, bub, naw. Which Griggs do ye call 'Pig-wigs?'"

" Why — *Pig-wigs*," Rufe reiterated obviously.

Then he explained. "He air Nate's nevy. He air Nate's oldest brother's biggest boy, — though he ain't sizable much. He air 'bout haffen ez big ez me — ef that," he added reflectively, thinking that even thus divided he had represented Pig-wigs as more massive than the facts justified.

"Ye see," he continued, "one day when his uncle Tim war over hyar ter the tanyard, I gin him one o' my game deedies ; an' ez soon ez he got home he showed 'em all that thar deedie — powerful, spryest poultry ye ever see! "

Rufe smiled ecstatically as only a chicken fancier can.

"An' Pig-wigs war plumb *de*-stracted fur a deedie too. An' he run all the way over hyar ter git me ter gin him one. But the deedies hed all gone ter bed, an' the old hen war hoverin' of 'em, an' I did n't want ter 'sturb 'em," said Rufe considerately. "So I tole Pig-wigs ter meet me at the tanyard early, an' I 'd fetch him one. An' ez his granny war goin' visitin' her married daughter, she let him ride behind her on thar sorrel mare ez fur ez the tanyard.

So he got hyar 'fore I did. An' I kem an' gin him the deedie."

Rufe paused abruptly, as if, having narrated this important transaction, he had exhausted the interest of the subject.

Byers was about to speak, but the tanner with a gesture repressed him.

"Ye hain't tole 'bout the pit an' the grant yit, bubby," he reminded the small boy.

Byers's display of impatience was not lost upon Rufe, and it added to the general acrimony of their relations.

"Waal," the small boy began alertly, "we-uns hed the deedie behind the smoke-house thar, an' I seen *him* " — Rufe pointed at Byers with disfavor — " a-comin' powerful slow inter the tanyard, an' I whispered ter Pig-wigs Griggs ter be quiet, an' not let *him* know ez we-uns war thar, 'kase he war always a-jawin' at me, 'thout the tanner war by ter keep him off'n me. So we-uns bided thar till *he* went inter the smoke-house. An' then ez we-uns kem by the shed, Pig-wigs seen his uncle Nate's coat hangin' on a peg thar, 'kase that thar

triflin' Tim hed furgot, an' lef' it thar when he
went ter see the deedies. An' Pig-wigs Griggs,
he 'lowed he knowed the coat war his uncle
Nate's by the favior of it, an' he reckoned the
paper stickin' out'n the pocket war the grant he
hed hearn Nate talkin' 'bout. An' I whispered
ter him ez he hed better ondertake ter tote it
home ter Nate. An' Pig-wigs said he could n't
tote the coat, bein' so lumbered up with the
deedie. But he would tote the grant in one
hand an' the deedie in t'other. He could n't
put the deedie in one o' his pockets, 'kase his
mother sews 'em all up, bein' ez he *would*
kerry sech a passel o' heavy truck in 'em, —
rocks an' sech, reg'lar bowlders," added Rufe,
with a casual remembrance of the museum in
his own pockets. " So Pig-wigs's mother sewed
'em all up, 'kase she said they war tore out all
the time, an' she seen no sense in a boy hevin'
a lot o' slits in his clothes ter let in the air
slanchwise on him. An' Pig-wigs 'lowed he 'd
tote the grant ef I would git it fur him. An'
I did."

" How did you-uns reach up ter that thar

peg?" demanded Byers, pointing to the peg
on which the coat had hung, far beyond Rufe's
reach.

"Clumb up on the wooden horse," said
Rufe promptly. "I peeked through the chinkin' an' seen ye thar a-smokin' yer pipe over
the fire."

Rufe winked audaciously, suddenly convin-
cing Byers as to the possessor of the big black
eyes, which he had recognized as characteristic
of the Dicey family, when they had peered
through the chinking.

" Waal, how did the grant git inter the pit,
Rufe, an' what hev become of it?" asked Byers, overlooking these personalities, for he felt
a certain anxiety in the matter, being the last
person known to have seen the grant, which,
by reason of his delay and indecision, had again
been spirited away.

" Pig-wigs put it thar, I tell ye," reiterated
Rufe. " Ye see, I hed got outside o' the gate,
an' Pig-wigs war a good ways behind, walkin'
toler'ble slow, bein' ez he hed ter kerry the
grant in one hand an' the deedie in t'other.

An' thar I see a-cropin' along on the ground a young rabbit — reg'lar baby rabbit. An' I motioned ter Pig-wigs ter come quick — I hed fund suthin'. An' ez Pig-wigs could n't put the deedie down, he laid the grant on top o' the boards ez kivered the pit. But the wind war brief, an' kem mighty nigh blowin' that grant away. So Pig-wigs jes' stuck it down 'twixt two planks, an' kem ter holp me ketch the rabbit. But Pig-wigs warn't no 'count ter holp. An' the rabbit got away. An' whilst Pig-wigs war foolin' round, he drapped his deedie, an' stepped on it — tromped the life out'n it." Rufe's expression was of funereal gravity. "An' then he follered me every foot o' the way home, beggin' an' beggin' me ter gin him another. But I would n't. I won't gin no more o' my deedies ter be tromped on, all round the mounting."

Rufe evidently felt that the line must be drawn somewhere.

"An' what hev gone with that thar grant? 'T war hyar yestiddy."

"I dunno," responded Rufe, carelessly.

" Mebbe Pig-wigs reminded hisself 'bout'n it arter awhile, an' kem an' got it."

This proved to be the case. For Andy Byers concerned himself enough in the matter to ride the old mule over to Nate's home, to push the inquiries. Nate was just emerging from the door. The claybank mare, saddled and bridled, stood in front of the cabin. He was evidently about to mount.

" Look-a-hyar, ye scamp ! " Byers saluted him gruffly, " why n't ye let we-uns know ez ye hed got back that thar grant o' yourn, ez hev sot the whole mounting catawampus? Pig-wigs hearn ye talkin' 'bout it at las', and tole ye ez he hed it, I s'pose ? "

Nate affected to examine the saddle-girth. He looked furtively over the mare's shoulder at Andy Byers. He could not guess how much of the facts had been developed. In sheer perversity he was tempted to deny that he had the grant. But Byers was a heavy man of scant patience, and he wore a surly air that boded ill to a trifler.

Nate nodded admission.

" Pig-wigs fotched it home, eh?" demanded Byers, leaning downward.

Once more Nate lifted his long, thin questioning face. His craft had no encouragement.

" Ef ye be minded to call him ' Pig-wigs '— his right name air Benjymen — 't war him ez fotched it home."

" Now ye air a mighty cantankerous, quar'l-some, aggervatin' critter!" Byers broke out irritably. "Ain't ye 'shamed o' this hyar hurrah ye hev kicked up fur nuthin'? accusin' o' Birt wrongful, an' sech?"

"Naw; I ain't 'shamed o' nuthin'!" said Nate hardily, springing into the saddle. " I 'm a-ridin' ter the Settle*mint* ter git word from the assayer 'bout'n the gold ez I hev fund. An'. when I rides back I 'll be wuth more'n enny man in the mountings or Sparty either!"

And he gave the mare the whip, and left Andy Byers, with his mouth full of rebukes, sitting motionless on the dozing old mule.

The mare came back from the Settlement late that night under lash and spur, at a speed

she had never before made. Day was hardly
astir when Nate Griggs, wild-eyed and hag-
gard, appeared at the tanyard in search of Birt.
He was loud with reproaches, for the assayer
had pronounced the "gold" only worthless
iron pyrites. He had received, too, a jeering
letter from his proposed partner in Sparta, who
had found sport in playing on his consequen-
tial ignorance and fancied sharpness. And
now Nate declared that Birt, also, had known
that the mineral was valueless, and had from
the first befooled him. In some way he
would compel Birt to refund all the money
that had been expended. How piteous was
Nate as he stood and checked off, on his trembling fingers, the surveyor's fee, the entry-
taker's fee, the register's fee, the secretary of
State's fee, the assayer's fee — Oh, ruin, ruin!
And what had he to show for it! a tract of
crags and chasms and precipitous gravelly
slopes and gullies worth not a mill an acre!
And this was all — for the office of laughing-
stock has no emoluments. Where was Birt?
He would hold Birt to account.

Andy Byers, listening, thought how well it was for Birt that Nate no longer had the loss of the grant as a grievance.

Perkins mysteriously beckoned Nate aside.

"Nate," he said in a low voice, "Birt air powerful mad 'bout that thar accusin' him o' stealin' the grant, when 't war some o' yer own folks, 'Pigwigs,' ez hed it all the time. I seen him goin' 'long towards yer house a leetle while ago. I reckon he air lookin' fur you. He hed that big cowhide, ez I gin him t'other day, in one hand. Ye jes' take the road home, an' ye 'll ketch up with him sure."

Nate's wits were in disastrous eclipse. Could he deduce nothing from the tanner's grin? He spent the day at the Settlement without ostensible reason, and only at nightfall did he return home, and by a devious route, very different from that indicated by Jubal Perkins.

Inquiry developed the fact that the boundaries of Nate's land did not include the salt lick, and his talents as an obstructer were not called into play. The professor was free to

dig as he chose for the antique bones he
sought, and many a long day did he and Birt
spend in this sequestered spot, with the great
crags towering above and the darkling vistas
of the ravine on either hand. There was a
long stretch of sunny weather, and somehow
that shifting purple haze accented all its lan-
guorous lustres. It seemed a vague sort of
poetry a-loose in the air, and color had license.
The law which decreed that a leaf should be
green was a dead letter. How gallantly red
and yellow they flared ; and others, how ten-
derly pink, and gray, and purplish of hue!
What poly-tinted fancies underfoot in the
moss ! Strange visitants came from the north.
Flocks of birds, southward bound, skimmed
these alien skies. Sometimes they alighted on
the tree-tops or along the banks of the torrent,
chattering in great excitement, commenting
mightily on the country.

Birt had never been so light-hearted as during these days. The cessation of anxiety was
itself a sort of happiness. The long, hard
ordeal to which the truth had subjected him
had ended triumphantly.

" Mighty onexpected things happen in this worl'," he said, reflectively. " It 'pears powerful cur'ous to me, arter all ez hev come an' gone, ez *I* ain't no loser by that thar gold mine down the ravine."

He himself was surprised that he did not rejoice in Nate's mortification and defeat. But somehow he had struck a moral equilibrium ; in mastering his anger and thirst for revenge, he had gained a stronger control of all the more unworthy impulses of his nature.

Meantime there was woe at the tanyard. Jube Perkins had been anxious to have Birt resume his old place on the old terms. The professor, however, would not release the boy from his engagement. It seemed that this man of science could deduce subtle distinctions of character in the mere wielding of a spade. He had never seen, he said, any one dig so conscientiously and so intelligently as Birt. The tanner suddenly found that conscience might prove a factor even in so simple a matter as driving the old mule around the bark-mill. The boy who had taken Birt's place was

13

a sullen, intractable fellow, and brutal. When
he yelled and swore and plied the lash, the old
mule would occasionally back his ears. The
climax came one day when the rash boy kicked
the animal. Now this reminded the mild-mannered old mule of his own youthful prowess
as a kicker. He revived his reputation. He
seemed to stand on his fore-legs and his muzzle, while his hind-legs played havoc behind
him. The terrified boy dared not come near
him. The bark-mill itself was endangered.
Jube Perkins had not done so much work for
a twelvemonth as in his efforts to keep the
boy, the mule, and the bark-mill going together.

There were no "finds" down by the lick to
rejoice the professor, and he went away at last
boneless, except in so far as nature had pro-
vided him. He left Birt amply rewarded for
his labor. So independent did Mrs. Dicey
feel with this sum of money in reserve, that
she would not agree that Birt should work on
the old terms with the tanner. Birt was dismayed by this temerity. Once more, however,

he recognized her acumen, for Jubal Perkins, although he left the house in a huff, came back again and promised good wages. Ignorant and simple as she was, her keen instinct for her son's best interest, his true welfare, endowed her words with wisdom. Thenceforth he esteemed no friend, no ally, equal to his mother.

It delighted him to witness her triumph in the proof of his innocence, and indeed she did not in this matter bear herself with meekness. It made him feel so prosperous to note her relapse into her old caustic habit of speech. Ah, if he were hurt or sore beset, every word would be tenderness.

Birt shortly compassed a much desired object. The mule's revival of his ancient glories as a "turrible kicker" had injured his market value, and Birt's earnings enabled him to purchase the animal at a low price. The mule lived to a great age, always with his master as " mild-mannered " as a lamb.

For some time Birt saw nothing of Nate, but one day the quondam friends met face to face on a narrow, precipitous path on the mountain side. Abject fear was expressed in Nate's sharp features, for escape was impossible.

There was no need of either fear or flight.

" How air ye, I'on Pyrite!" cried Birt cheerfully.

The martyr's countenance changed.

" Ye never done me right 'bout that thar mine, Birt Dicey," Nate said reproachfully. " Ye mus' hev knowed from the fust ez them thar rocks war good fur nuthin'."

"Ye air the deceivinest sandy-headed Pyrite that ever war on the top o' this mounting, an' ye knows it," Birt retorted in high good humor; " an' ef it war wuth my while I 'd gin ye a old-fashion larrupin' jes' ter pay ye fur the trick ez ye played on me. But I ain't keerin' fur that, now. Stan' back thar, Tennessee ! "

Since then, Tennessee, always preserving the influence she wielded that memorable night, has grown to be a woman — never pretty, but, as her brother still stoutly avers, " powerful peart."

www.ingramcontent.com/pod-product-compliance
Lightning Source LLC
Chambersburg PA
CBHW031058280326
41928CB00049B/968